UNITING A DIVIDED NATION

Political Extremism in America

Ray William Thion

Contacts:
X: @raywthion53591
Email: raywilliamthion@gmail.com

ISBN: 979-8-9953063-1-3

Printed in the United States.

Table of Contents

Introduction

It's the evening, and your kitchen table is loaded with bills. Your phone is going off with alerts about our politicians' failures. Government shutdowns, rising prices, healthcare premiums increasing - and they just gave themselves another raise. You lean back, rub your tired eyes, and sigh, wondering if anyone in government even remembers what it feels like to make ends meet. Does anyone care about the grinding exhaustion that follows you into every day? The kind where you wonder if you'll ever catch a break? Something is off in our politics, and everyone feels it.

What you are about to read is a blueprint of hope for you, the American moderate. It is a book for the politically isolated, the disillusioned, the politically homeless. For you who keep shouting into the void, wondering if anyone's even listening. It is a blueprint for you on the actions you can take and how you can put an end to the extremism and political polarization that is destabilizing our country, and initiate a return to common sense and moderation.

It is a call for a peaceful revolution, a call for you to rise, raise your voice, and provide practical, implementable steps to succeed in doing so. It is a call for action - not for you to increase as you already have: through protests demanding justice and other actions you have rightfully taken on behalf of justice. Instead, it is a call, a guide for additional alternate steps you can take for successful and lasting change.

The solution proposed here is not another political work citing the apparent problems that are plaguing our nation without any proposed hope for a solid implementable solution, nor is it a call for the obvious or usual actions you have heard time and time again like "go to the streets," "protest," "voice your concerns," "vote and get your friends and family to go vote," "every vote matters." While protest, voting, and other actions are necessary, this work goes beyond what you already know to be true and the actions you have taken.

It educates you on additional steps you can take to more effectively guarantee your success in achieving significant and lasting social change. These are proven, implementable steps, a guide that will empower you to elevate your voice to where it can't be ignored any longer, a way to command the attention of the leaders that work for you, steps you can take to dictate fair and just change in our fracturing democracy, a blueprint on how to return power to where it should reside: in you.

We are at one of the most critical moments in history. We are on the cusp of a great abyss, and we keep edging ever forward with increasing speed. It seems that we are powerless to stop; it seems inevitable that we are about to take our last steps into a pit of apocalyptic darkness. We are about to destroy ourselves, our time is running out, and it seems we can't avoid it. Time is slipping through our fingers like sand, and the weight of what's coming presses on your chest. You're not imagining how grave this moment feels.

The world is a powder keg about to explode. The global geopolitical situation is more unstable than it has ever been; wars ranging from Europe to the Middle East and even Asia threaten international security. Economic uncertainty and instability are now destabilizing even the world's biggest economies. Global debt has reached an all-time high, threatening a financial catastrophe that many experts warn would dwarf the Great Depression.

Western nations are experiencing unprecedented political, social, and cultural polarity and conflict.

Executed and attempted political assassinations of the most senior leaders and figures have been on the rise. According to some experts, climate change is at the point of no return.

Many nations around the world are experiencing an unprecedented level of political, economic, and social fracturing and chaos. The country that is leading in this is also the nation with the title of the world leader, the global hegemon, the most significant architect of the current international order: the United States of America.

One of the most fascinating yet confusing aspects of the American experiment is its irony. The years of endless contradiction in people's behavior. For years, despite America's massive, seeming hypocrisy, despite America's political chaos, even though many Americans are unable to find a representative that truly represents their interests because of the two-party binary, both individuals who hate America and love her, individuals who have risen to the very top in this experiment accumulating unimaginable wealth and prosperity, and individuals who feel they have been cheated and exploited by the 1%, individuals who hold vastly different ideals and views about the world all agree on one thing: participation in her political process.

"We hold these truths to be self-evident, that all men are created equal, that their Creator endows them with certain unalienable Rights, that among these are Life, Liberty, and the pursuit of Happiness."

This quote expresses the founders' vision, the blueprint for a nation of freedom, equality, and prosperity for everyone. But this nation hasn't come into existence. At least not yet. A society that truly embodies the ideals perhaps the world's most incredible group of political geniuses set out to achieve at the founding has never come to fruition. From the very beginning of American history, a massive portion of the population was enslaved. The rights of women were limited, and other human rights and freedoms were to some extent not fully realized.

None of this makes the American experiment hypocritical. The Founding Fathers were very aware of slavery in the country. That meant that the rights and freedoms they envisioned were not fully realized. However, the spirit and ideas of the time limited the wiggle room they had to make changes. Despite the genius of their ideas, they were limited by the spirit and ideas of the time.

I don't think the founders were setting up a nation so much as a system. The founders weren't setting up a nation that truly embodied freedom, equality, and perfect justice for all; they were setting up a system that would one day create such a nation. They were setting up a system built on free speech, checks and balances, and the protection of rights and freedoms to as large a group as prevailing culture and attitudes would allow at the time.

A system built in such a way that it would allow American heroes later on - such as Abraham Lincoln, Harriet Tubman, Martin Luther King, John F. Kennedy, Ronald Reagan, and many other American heroes - to finish the work that they started, to use this genius of a system to further these human ideals, and prove to the world that a nation of true freedom, genuine equality, and true justice can be achieved.

For years, this system has been moving forward. America, for most of its history, has increasingly become a freer, democratic, inclusive, and human rights-based nation. But something unusual has happened recently. For the first time in her history, this system has not only stagnated but also gone backward. Furthermore, contrary to what intuition would have you believe, it is not just old, persistent views on the right that have caused its decline, but new views on the left that have become so fanatical that they are also the cause of the slowdown in progress.

For the first time in American history, the system the founders created is in crisis. The dream, the vision that the founders set for a nation of freedom, justice, equality - a beacon of democracy - is now at risk of never becoming realized.

Without a doubt, the founders were the most incredible group of political geniuses in history, far ahead of their time in their understanding of the social sciences. During the founding, they covered every loophole. They addressed any loose ends to ensure that it would be challenging to corrupt American democracy with tyranny, that it would remain a free nation, consistently progressing forward, becoming a more equal, just, and free society.

The United States holds the title as a nation of freedom, a land of unparalleled opportunity and prosperity, a land where the individual can live their dream life, and the world's only beacon of democracy.

But ask yourself - are you really living that dream? I'm not just talking about saving up to get that car you have been wanting, or getting a promotion at your job. I'm talking about the real life of your dreams, the American dream. Are you enjoying not just financial security, but what the American dream promised: financial prosperity? This prosperity was enjoyed in the 50s, 60s, and 70s in America, where a young adult could easily buy their first home. Do you feel you live in the greatest democracy in the world, the democratic beacon, where your vote, your voice, actually has a meaningful impact?

In 1790, a US House member represented around 57,169 Americans; today that number has grown to 747,184. Obviously, this would pose significant challenges for any single representative to properly understand the concerns and accurately represent such a large group of people as the founders intended for a U.S. House Representative at the beginning.

In 2024, a mere 7% of voters decided a massive 87% of the U.S. House of Representatives. True Democrats and Republicans, excluding independents who are forced to register just to participate, represent less than 40% of the American voting population, but determine nearly 100% of election outcomes.

The two-party binary system makes it impossible for any third party or an independent candidate to succeed. Closed primaries silence the voice of millions of Americans who are excluded from the election system for not aligning with one of the two major parties. Gerrymandering (the manipulation of electoral district lines to favor specific election outcomes) gives political parties massive advantages at the expense of American voters' voices.

Both parties have gone (and continue to go) more extreme in their ideology, alienating and becoming disconnected from the average American voter.

The average American does not have a voice because when you take away somebody's ability to choose, you also take away their voice, and that is precisely what the two-party system does. The two-party system only benefits a small group of fanatics on the extreme right and left while taking away the voice of the millions of other Americans who desperately long for alternative, less extreme options.

Because of all of this, America of today is much less democratic than it once was. Most Americans are ruled by a small group of right-wing and left-wing extremists who have molded the election system only to benefit themselves.

Therefore, things like economic instability, rising inflation, the increasing cost of healthcare, and the numerous other problems everyday Americans face can all be traced back to the extremism in the two-party system. Politicians tend to represent their base, and right now, the vast majority of the base of elected leaders is a small minority of extremists on the left and the right. Due to polarization, the problems and challenges the vast majority of Americans face are utterly foreign to them.

During election campaigns, both sides claim they hold America's interests - your interests - at heart, to represent you, and promise to implement change. The Biden election campaign ran on a promise of centrism, to unite America and bring back moderation and compromise.

But once in office, it proved to be the most far-left extremist administration in American history, going so far as to directly or indirectly support things like sterilizing and performing sex change surgeries on children unable to consent, taking away parents' rights in the process.

The Trump campaign ran on "common sense" and promised to unite America. But instead, the same division and political polarity that existed before he got elected and even during his first term still exist today.

The Trump campaign promised to revive the American economy and reverse years of economic damage caused by unsound Woke-Socialist policies, such as reckless spending. But the One Big Beautiful Bill is one of, if not the biggest, spending bills in American history, estimated to add a massive $3.4 trillion to the U.S. debt over the next decade, which would massively increase inflation and economic instability.

If the debt and inflation weren't bad enough, the bill also dramatically reduces welfare benefits, including cuts to Medicaid, food assistance, and other programs that millions of Americans rely on.

The bill increases the cost of healthcare and other services Americans desperately rely on because of inflation. Still, it cuts the monetary assistance needed to acquire these services.

Both sides attack the other for straying from American ideals and for violating and disregarding the Constitution. The truth is that both sides, left and right, Republican and Democrat, have strayed away from the founding ideals of our nation, and both sides continue to disregard the Constitution.

The right has gone so far extreme that they display characteristics similar to fascism. The left has become so fanatical that the ideology that was once the ideology of equality, fairness, and acceptance has now developed into the ideology of discrimination, intolerance, and violence, as seen through beliefs such as revenge racism and sexism.

Both sides have very little tolerance for views that run counter to their increasingly extreme beliefs. Both sides have become more radical and are not willing to compromise, leading to the political instability and chaos we see in America today.

The American people are disillusioned, politically isolated, and the institutions that once represented them - that were their voice, furthered their will, and held their interests and concerns - have now abandoned them in favor of their own interests, extreme radicals, and special interests.

Democrats take the extreme position of wanting open borders, while Republicans take the other extreme of separating immigrant families. Many Democrats support sterilization and sex change for children. In contrast, many Republicans have taken the other extreme by proposing legislation to severely limit or ban the rights of America's LGBTQ community.

Many Americans are experiencing financial and economic insecurity caused by unsound Democratic economic policies, while at the same time losing welfare benefits like Medicare and food assistance because of Republicans.

As both sides become increasingly extreme, they abandon reason and common sense.

In reality, your vote is not for a representative of your choosing; your vote is a tiebreaker between two warring Democratic and Republican factions.

You are just a tool to be humored during election campaigns so a tiebreaker vote can be attained. Once they get into office, your needs, your struggles, your worries, and concerns are all but forgotten.

The point is that our system is not only in trouble, but many experts have consistently warned that we are on the verge of the most significant political, social, and economic crisis in history. This crisis would dwarf the Soviet Union's collapse in 1991.

Our political system is more corrupt and dysfunctional than it has ever been, our national debt is at its highest point in history, threatening economic collapse, social unrest is on the rise, and politicians on both the left and the right have gone so extreme that they have called for or even committed political violence and rioting. We have seen some of the boldest attempted as well as executed political assassinations of the most senior leaders in our nation.

All of this is going on while the two major political parties seem only to be concerned with special interests and pleasing their most radical constituents, abandoning the average American voter in the process.

This unprecedented social war going on in our country right now can be described as a never-ending deadlock between two small groups of radicals on the left and right who have consolidated power.

Their end goal is to destroy the other and take complete control of American society, which would enable them to implement their most radical agendas without any constraints.

At the end of the day, it is not the left-wing or right-wing radical extremists - but it is the average, day-to-day American, you, who is forced to pay the highest price. You pay the price for rising inflation, the rising cost of healthcare. You have to deal with the consequences of a government shutdown and social unrest. It is hard-working Americans who face the risk of losing Social Security if it goes bankrupt due to reckless spending.

You're the one carrying the weight of all this chaos.

This book isn't going to talk about the need for a third party or a third-party candidate, the need for compromise, or how to unite America. This book is going to go much deeper than that.

It will reveal the root causes of these issues, the causes of disunity, and the reason why third political options consistently achieve little success or fail.

We will then present a surprisingly simple solution to this serious problem. This solution is so obvious, so sensible, a solution that, in itself, embodies the most basic ideals on which American democracy is based, that you will wonder why it wasn't one of the first things implemented during the early stages of American history.

This solution will end the increasing political extremism and bring back moderation, centrism, unity, and compromise.

This is actually practical, something that can be implemented to finally fix the problems our democracy faces and bring back the voice of the American voter.

This solution will not only allow third, fourth, or even fifth options to succeed, but also any party or candidate chosen by the people.

It will re-implement a genuinely democratic system, something that will protect democracy from the threat of two-party political monopoly and ensure that ultimate power rests not in the hands of special interests or extremist groups, but in the hands of the legitimate sovereign: the people.

I produced this work because I'm tired; I am so tired of it all: the constant fighting with no end in sight, the protests with no significant or lasting change, the endless political polarity and bickering, the racism, the intolerance, the apathy toward the less fortunate.

This will not go on forever without consequence. We have to end it, because if we don't, we're going to destroy ourselves. We must unite and put our differences aside.

If we stand any chance of averting this course of destruction, chaos, corruption, and injustice, we must tolerate each other once again. We must stop judging a person's beliefs or worldview as right or wrong; instead, you must look at a person's character as good or evil, their intention as honest or corrupt. Only then can we unite. Because nothing in the universe is more unstoppable than the irresistible force of the will, passion, and determination of noble-hearted men and women. It was the same passion and will that built this nation: George Washington, James Madison, Harriet Tubman, Abraham Lincoln, Amelia Earhart, Martin Luther King, and countless other historical figures as well as the unknown individuals whose names are etched in silence. All of these individuals played a role in building this great nation.

Look at all we have accomplished! Our nation is nothing short of a miracle. From the final song sung in unison at the Grammys, to the inspiring speeches of hope from Martin Luther King, national heroes such as George Washington, Abraham Lincoln, Harriet Tubman, and Chris Kyle, to the famed names of celebrities known around the world like Elvis Presley, Marilyn Monroe, Tom Cruise - this nation is nothing short of a miracle of human brilliance.

It's because when you unleash the chains of dogma, obstinacy, and outdated unreasonable traditions, when you allow men, women, and people of different groups, backgrounds, and uniqueness to be free, when you let the dreamer dream and the manifester manifest, they will create magic that will go on to change the world for generations to come.

Our land is a place where dreams become manifested, where ideas become reality, and where unreasonable hopes defy reason and probability; because will and passion is stronger than the rigidness of practicality and the mountain of possibility of obstacles. Our (true) nation and its (real ideals it was founded on) is a land of acceptance, difference, freedom, and equality. A land of heroes and inspirers, and the inspired who become the next generation of inspirational heroes. A land of success and opportunity, a nation of people looked up to, an example to the world of what we as humans can accomplish when we all, despite being different and individually unique, unite under one flag of human spirit.

You must not let this beautiful miracle die, fade away into the fog of extremism. We have accomplished so much, and extremists on the right and the left are actively ruining all we have achieved, eroding the legacy of American heroes of the past. They want to implement their failed ideology: the ideals of prejudice, revenge, and racism. They want to replace freedom with tyranny, equality with division, openness with their closed-minded failed worldviews.

They want to take us backward into old outdated ways of the past; they want to hold on to ideas and principles that history has proven lead to poverty and economic decline. Instead of recovery and healing from the wounds of the past, the radical left wants to reopen these wounds through revenge and reverse prejudice of certain groups for sins they never committed; the guilt of these condemned groups lies not in the crime of action, but in the crime of look, because their skin, their eye color is the same as the criminal of racism and bigotry in the past - they too must also be guilty of the crime.

While the left is intent on hate-motivated revenge, the far right is working to reinstate the old social institutions of oppression, the historical hierarchies of discrimination, the backward values of bigotry.

We are in dark times. This beacon of the American spirit has grown dim. Things are arguably worse than they have ever been. But there shines a glimmer of hope. The light of the American spirit is dim, but it is not out. We must do all we can to preserve this fading, glimmering light of this grand experiment, because it is humanity's only hope. Because if we lose the light of freedom, the beacon of the blessings of liberty here in this land, this will be the last hope of humanity on earth. Where will humanity go? Where will she look to for the dreams, blessings, and prosperity; the magic of human excellence?

CHAPTER 1:

The Search for the Crack in Democracy

The 60s were a time of seemingly endless instability. There were political assassinations, a close call on a nuclear apocalypse in Cuba, the Vietnam War, the hippie movement, the battle for civil rights, humans went to the moon, the sexual revolution, and the feminist movement. The changes challenged the most basic assumptions of society. In retrospect, the 60s embodied the vast potential humanity has for creativity and progress. But they also revealed the appetite for death and destruction.

Some twenty years later, it appeared that much of this strife had ended as the world experienced what some mistakenly called the "end of history." After the fall of the Soviet Union, China liberalized parts of its economy, and democratization was occurring in what had previously been known as the third world; that global ideological struggle seemed to be a thing of the past. Grand debates between religious, political, and other ideologies were believed to be finally over. The onward march of liberalism, joined by globalization, created what seemed like an unstoppable tide. It appeared to most observers that liberalism would win and the entire world would end up under the same system.

Not everyone shared the optimism. But few believed that another era of social and political conflict, world turmoil, and chaos was in the cards.

But we know how it turned out. The 2020s have been ridiculously dramatic eras in human history. This era is a definitive one, with far-reaching consequences. We have seen dramatic changes, ranging from a pandemic that brought the world to a standstill to the popularization of culturally controversial phenomena like OnlyFans. At the same time, geopolitical tensions have produced a new Cold War. The threat of nuclear apocalypse remains potent, but is now joined by potentially destructive forms of warfare such as cyber attacks, drones, and artificial intelligence. The West is experiencing a social, cultural, and political revolution that we don't really understand. As has often been the case, ground zero for much of this change is the United States of America, the country we like to think of as a bastion of democracy.

The centrality of this country is not always a good thing. Problems are mounting. Most notably, America is more polarized than it has been since the Civil War. An economic crisis driven by seemingly unsustainable levels of debt is highly likely. After all, interest payments on the debt consume an unsustainable share of the federal budget.

Meanwhile, the political system has turned increasingly unrepresentative. Due to the ills of the primary system, representatives pander to the extremists in our population. That leaves most regular Americans unrepresented. The two main parties compound the problem. The Democrats and Republicans have made it virtually impossible for a third party to compete. That leaves the American people's thirst for new ideas and leadership unquenched. Even within the parties, opposition to ideological extremism is suppressed. As a result of these developments, the vast majority of the American population is deprived of an authentic voice.

The failure of third parties isn't just the fault of the big two. It is also due to shortcomings among the challengers. Moderate political movements have failed to identify the root of America's problems. They are, of course, aware of the symptoms. The political chaos, disunity, and culture wars are apparent to all. But they don't seem to grasp the real causes of these maladies.

Identifying a problem and getting to the bottom of it are entirely different things. Strong definitions and a proper understanding of what we face are needed to formulate actual solutions. We are on a dangerous path. With an understanding of the core problems, we can slow it down and even reverse it.

There is a singular cause to all of these problems. If you allow me, I will show you how every single problem America faces is tied to one core issue that is weakening the very fabric of our democracy. To understand that, we need to grasp the force shaping human behavior - and, by extension, society itself. That force is every individual's system of beliefs: their deeply held values and overarching ideology.

What is Ideology?

The term ideology was initially coined by the French philosopher Antoine Destutt de Tracy. He used two Greek words: idea and logia, meaning idea or concept, and study or science, to create this term. So the etymological meaning of the word is the science or study of ideas or concepts. Ideologies can be separated into six major categories: Political, Economic, Religious, Philosophical, Social, and Cultural.

Furthermore, ideology can be defined as a system of ideas a person holds and attaches their heart to that gives them meaning and purpose, a way of interpreting reality, a way of understanding oneself, a justification for behaviour, a thing that creates allegiance and worship, and how to live, as well as other things. These ideas can be beliefs or interpretations, rules or laws a person holds, principles, or other forms of ideas.

Specific ideological ideas that fall in the belief category are believing in God and the devil, believing in evolution and the Big Bang, believing in a simulated universe, and so on. Ideological principles and laws can be things such as freedom, human rights, the scientific method, equality, racial superiority, gender or sexual superiority, worshiping god and so on.

Some ideologies' ideas are objective facts, while others are theoretical. Then others are subjective personal truths, beliefs, or other subjective ideas.

People often confuse ideology and philosophy because they share similarities. A good way to illustrate the difference is by using theology as an example. Theology deals with ideas and concepts related to spirituality, divinity, God, and religion. All are derived from the power of faith. On the other hand, philosophy pertains to ideas stemming from wisdom. That can include the pursuit of truth regarding the nature of reality, existence, meaning, and purpose. In philosophy, reason and logic are pursued instead of faith. Ideology is broader, encompassing both theology and philosophy. Indeed, an ideology usually includes elements of both faith and wisdom arranged to support each other.

But it is a mistake to see ideology as primarily a matter of belief. It constitutes an integral part of individual identity - your ideology is your particular constitution, defining who you are and what you stand for. It is a symbolic meaning that flows through your veins. When you lose faith in your ideology, it can feel like a metaphorical and spiritual death. Ultimately, the key to meaning and happiness is to follow your heart. That is the ultimate guide to meaning, purpose, and joy. The path goes through our hearts. It's not perfect and will sometimes lead to pain or failure. However, if you stay committed - trusting your own experience while aligning with the world around you - you will discover your true purpose and unleash the immense power within you. At that point, the universe can seem to bend to your will, allowing you to shape your life and reality.

Whether you are an atheist or an evolutionist, a Christian who dedicates your life to Jesus Christ, or a Muslim committed to Allah, a patriot, or a person devoted to work, discipline, and self-improvement, every single one of those is a form of ideology - ideas a person holds within their heart. They provide a fundamental purpose that gives meaning; an individual constitution that defines people. But they also work on a broader level, guiding the paths of nations and, by extension, the course of history.

The Psychology of Ideology

Human decisions boil down to a fundamental push-and-pull of emotions: love and hate, pleasure and pain. Our lives are, to a great extent, motivated by an attempt to seek out what we love, while avoiding pain.

However, the forces of love and hate motivating our actions are not mutually exclusive. Every force in the universe has a polarity and an antithesis. People are led astray by this dynamic. They mistake love and hate for good and evil. They ascribe moral and immoral characteristics to these forces.

But these concepts are not moral or prescriptive. They are just emotions.

Love consists of the emotional attraction a conscious being feels toward a person or object, arising from the pleasure the person or object provides. Hate is the negative emotion one feels towards an object or person that causes stress, fear, or anger. The two cannot exist without the other, and are equally present in every situation. The amount of love you hold towards a person is equal to the hate you have towards what threatens them. In other words, the amount of love an individual holds is perfectly balanced by the hate in their hearts. For example, a soldier is willing to kill due to the patriotic love he has for his nation. The anger that motivates pulling the trigger and extinguishing a life derives from their patriotism. The man who loves God hates the devil by equal measure. It's a mental algorithm driven by two opposing emotional forces that ultimately shape every decision and action a person takes.

Ideology is motivated by psychological need. It is a mindset, more than anything else.

The emotional resonance of ideology can lead to immense human suffering. Take, for example, a particular infamous political ideology that arose in 1930s Germany and resulted in the genocide of millions while launching the deadliest, most destructive war in human history. But it can also be the cause of good things, such as national unity and mobilization for national or social causes, such as the abolition of slavery or the Civil Rights movement.

Ideology is the force that sets in motion great political programs. A schoolteacher in Germany didn't just wake up one day, decide he was going to go to a place called Auschwitz, strip men, women, and children naked, herd them into a gas chamber, and push a button that would eliminate the lives of hundreds of human beings in seconds. He took those actions after cultivating a particular set of ideas. The interpretation of reality inherent in the ideology these ideas produced justified the actions in his mind. That enabled him, and many others like him, to perform what they believed were "just" or "patriotic" acts.

That is the power of ideology. If you can convince a group of Germans in the 1930s that a specific group of humans is inferior, evil, and to blame for a nation's misfortunes, then you can get school teachers, doctors, fathers, and even young boys to commit themselves to genocide. But that same power can convince groups of people of the sacredness of human rights, democracy, and the rule of law, and to reject the evils of tyranny. The force is so compelling that it can convince mothers to send their own sons across oceans and risk their lives to fight fascism.

The most consequential decisions we make as nations and societies are determined by ideology. Each of these consists of countless ideological choices made by individuals. Times of social unrest, war, and peace and prosperity can all be traced back to this fundamental influence on human behavior. It is the conductor of the symphony of the human heart.

Political reality is an ideological battle of wills over which worldview will ultimately prevail. We are currently in a second Cold War between the ideology of liberal democracy and that of authoritarianism. Meanwhile, the social and cultural war plaguing liberal democratic nations is a battle between left-wing and right-wing extremists. Meanwhile, everyday people (who are mostly centrists and moderates) turn out to be the biggest victims. They are forced to pay the highest price despite having little say due to an electoral system that favors fanatics. Life is a battle, whether you are a nonhuman species or a human with evolved spirituality. Life is a struggle. It is, at heart, a battle of wills, and whoever has the strongest comes out on top.

Categories of Ideologies

Ideologies fall within broad categories, which in turn fall into even larger groupings. In the broadest sense, there are two main political categories: extremist and centrist. Extremist ideologies are those with strong components of violence, hatred, and intolerance. They harbor unjust prejudices against certain groups and cling to absolutist, intolerant beliefs, refusing to accept any ideas or viewpoints that differ from their own. Due to these factors, extremist ideas often violate others' rights and freedoms.

When I say someone is intolerant or absolutist, I don't mean they're wrong just for having different beliefs. Indeed, agreeing to disagree is part of tolerance. John Rawls, a foundational figure in modern liberal political philosophy, championed the idea of overlapping consensus. Rawls argued that in a liberal democracy, people with very different views can still agree on fundamental principles, since those principles are what guarantee the freedom to live according to their own values. In this context, an absolutist or intolerant person is someone who doesn't agree to disagree. Instead, they condemn those they disagree with to a point that leads to the suppression of free speech, persecution, and even violence.

As shown on the Ideological Compass - a tool that maps political beliefs along two axes (left–right) and (authoritarian–libertarian) - there are four major categories of extremism: left, right, authoritarian, and libertarian. Several ideologies can fall within each of these categories. Nonetheless, all the ideologies within a single category share a similar set of ideals and worldviews.

In general, ideologies on the extremist far right favor particularist views and support traditional or longstanding power structures. A particularist ideology favors the interests of a particular group at the expense of the general public or the greater good. Traditional forms of prejudice - such as racism, sexism, and other far-right biases - are rooted in historically dominant groups discriminating against or exerting control over those who have held less power. Traditional power structures include groups of individuals who have traditionally had more power or influence in society, such as the aristocracy, the wealthy, royal families, and racial groups associated with political advantage in a given society.

Absolute monarchism is often considered among the most extreme right-wing ideologies, as it concentrates all political power in the hands of a single, traditionally hereditary ruler. It is a particularly traditional power structure, since for much of human history, monarchs held ultimate power. It is also the most particularist because it is a system that favors the interests of one individual at the expense of all others.

As you move from the far right toward the center, you encounter ideologies that are less radical than absolute monarchism but are still forms of extremism. Ideologies here may favor broader swathes of society, like the aristocracy and other elites, over everyone else. Moving further from the extremes, the ideologies become less extreme and start to favor broader groups - often those who have had less power in society but who may still hold more influence than other marginalized groups. These are still particularistic to some extent, focusing on the interests of people from certain ethnicities, nationalities, or social classes that have been relatively more powerful compared to others.

On the other hand, far-left ideologies promote broad, generalist goals. To bring these priorities to fruition, they often seek to overturn existing power structures, sometimes replacing them with new systems or advocating redistribution of power as a form of redress or "revenge." By "generalist," I mean ideologies that claim to benefit the general public or a large collective of people, even if that entails sacrificing individual rights and freedoms for the purpose. Meanwhile, "revenge" in new power structures refers to a tendency toward prejudice or discrimination that flips the old hierarchy on its head. Put simply, this is the urge to respond to past injustices by perpetrating new ones against those who have lost their privilege. For example, some might argue that racial minorities have the right to discriminate against former oppressors, or that women can now push back against men to address past injustices of patriarchy. These are examples of far-left prejudice, where the response to old wrongs becomes a new form of discrimination.

"Woke-communism," a term sometimes used to describe the blend of radical social-justice activism and far-left economic ideas, stands at the furthest extreme of left-wing ideology. It is perhaps the most sweeping in its vision of social change and the most uncompromising in its justification of prejudice as payback for historical wrongs.

Ideology in Society

Ideology plays a crucial part in determining the structure of a given society and its relative success.

Take the United States, for example. The fundamental ideology that shaped American society is liberalism. Not the liberalism of the current-day Democratic Party or other modern left-wing groups in the West. Instead, it refers to the original meaning of liberalism: the Enlightenment-era ideology rooted in ideals like individual liberty, human rights, private property, justice, and democratic governance.

The central tenets of the American ideology stem from liberalism, a vital element of which is the belief that every individual has fundamental rights that no one, even the government, can violate. This element is enshrined in the constitution, which guarantees and protects these rights. To preserve these rights, liberalism holds that legitimate government rests on the consent of the governed - a central idea in American republicanism and a foundational one in many other democratic ideologies. In the American context, this takes the form of a system in which leaders are elected to represent the people and held accountable by them. The liberal belief in an individual's right to private property is expressed in the principles of free-market capitalism. The goal of this ideology is the creation of a free nation of free men and women, guaranteeing individuals' rights to exercise them and enjoy prosperity.

The societal pyramid shows the fundamental role ideology plays in society. At the top, ideology serves as the fundamental influence and defining blueprint behind a given society. Under that, you have the government and economy, which are shaped by ideology. At the bottom, prevailing culture and attitudes are derived from the government and economic systems.

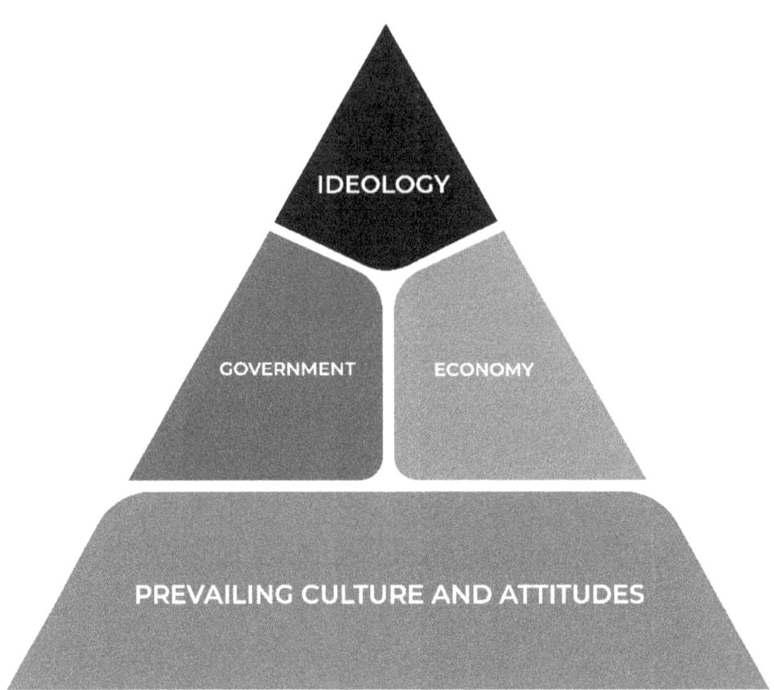

Whether it was the Soviet Union shaped by Marxism, Nazi Germany driven by fascism, or modern-day Iran guided by Islamic theocracy, every society's government, economy, structure, culture, and even its overall trajectory are rooted in a core ideology. This blueprint defines and shapes how that society functions.

A given society will not, as a rule, have more than one fundamental ideology. A nation trying to practice two forms of government or economic systems at once would end up facing chaos and dysfunction. A society needs to have one fundamental ideology, one fundamental belief system, and protect this system to avoid political and social fracturing.

While most forms of government have mechanisms to safeguard their core ideology, free and democratic societies often lack such protections. That point is, in fact, where liberal democracy is most vulnerable. I'll return to this point later.

The Results of Ideology

While laws are one crucial way an ideology is expressed in society, the actual results of an ideology come from how its core ideas are put into practice - in law, culture, institutions, and everyday life. For example, liberalism, the guiding ideology behind the U.S. Constitution, has helped produce the world's largest economy, technological leadership, the most powerful military in history, and far-reaching social and cultural influence. It has also contributed to periods of political division and gridlock, while making the United States the top destination for immigrants drawn by the promise of the American dream.

On the other hand, Marxism inspired the laws and formation of the USSR. The results were economic stagnation and ultimate collapse, with high technological advancement in narrow categories undermined by low technological advancement on broader levels. The USSR also experienced a mass exodus of citizens trying to leave, as they sought out free societies. There are countless other examples of the success and failure of societies due to the implementation of different ideologies.

The results of ideology are neither subjective nor theoretical. They are undeniable. To deny this is as unreasonable as rejecting the results of a well-established scientific experiment. So far, no other society has achieved the success of the United States and other free societies. The implementation of centrist ideologies has been central to this success.

As we have seen, the importance of pursuing centrist ideals is crucial to the stability of democracy. But that doesn't mean liberal democracy and centrist leadership fall far short of their ideals. Often spectacularly so. Think of the internment of Japanese American citizens during World War II, centuries of colonial oppression by the supposedly reasonable British Empire, or the genocide of natives in the United States, Canada, and Australia. Sometimes the idea of centrism acts as a cover for awful crimes.

But that is when leaders lose sight of what centrist values actually mean and go to excesses to fight those who espouse extremist views. Those pursuing centrism must not fall into that trap. Centrism is only as good as the values that it actively promotes. But even at their worst, centrist leaders do not commit the level of crimes that extremist regimes, on the right and left alike, commit.

What Laws Are

Laws in any society flow naturally from a particular ideology. They interpret ideology into discernible patterns of behavior. Laws in a liberal society with an orderly separation of powers are usually made by the legislative branch, and interpreted and judged by the judicial branch. Meanwhile, laws are enacted and enforced by the executive powers of government. From the laws of the constitution to regulations, state laws, and city ordinances, all laws are, or are inspired by, a particular system of ideas.

In constitutional forms of government, especially in the American Republic, any law that's passed must follow the framework and ideas laid out in the Constitution. Through this process, the ideas of a given ideology can filter through the constitution into the laws regulating the life of a nation. Even in countries without a single written constitution, laws are guided by foundational principles. They may derive from tradition, precedent, or longstanding legal frameworks. In all cases, these core ideas are essential to the formation and application of a nation's rules.

Centrism, the Antithesis of Extremism

We often talk about right-wing and left-wing extremism. Infamous forms of right-wing extremism, such as the Nazis in Germany, or left-wing extremism such as the communist Soviet Union, come to mind. But you never hear about centrist extremism. It is a direct contradiction, much like saying "Communist Nazi." The meanings of these two words are mutually exclusive, since centrist ideology by definition stays away from the extremes.

It is the extremist ideas that violate human rights and freedoms. For example, absolute monarchs and their collaborators violated human rights because of their particularist view that the monarch possesses divine rights, rendering them superior to others. Meanwhile, right-wing racism comes from the particularist view that a particular race is superior to others and has the right to discriminate against so-called "inferior races."

On the extremist left, communists believe in ideals that violate a person's right to property. They view the rights of the general public as more important than those of the individual.

Moving upward on the ideological compass, we find authoritarianism and autocratic rule. When one individual or a small group holds absolute power, it inevitably limits or denies individual rights and personal liberty. This approach inevitably silences the people. When all power is concentrated at the top, ordinary citizens lose their voice and have no real say over their own lives or the direction of society.

The autocrat exploits the nation's resources for personal gain.

Moving to anarchism - this is its own form of extremism. In the society it envisions, there is no rule of law or government. Most forms of anarchism envision alternative systems of voluntarily organized cooperation. They seek a society based on communal decision-making and mutual accountability. But without a government to enforce that, it is likely that each group, or even each individual, will decide for themselves what's right. This creates a system in which chaos reigns, and the strongest prevail. That is an extreme outcome.

So if the goal is to build a society that balances the needs of the individual with those of society, does not violate the rights and freedoms of the individual to accommodate the majority, and does not pursue a repressive or non-existent government, the only option is centrism. This is because centrism is not overly particularist, nor is it overly generalist. Power is not excessively concentrated, nor is it excessively dispersed. Centrism is a position that fits all groups and individuals, where compromise, discourse, and common sense prevail. An equilibrium that rejects the polarity, hostility, and chaos that extremism entails.

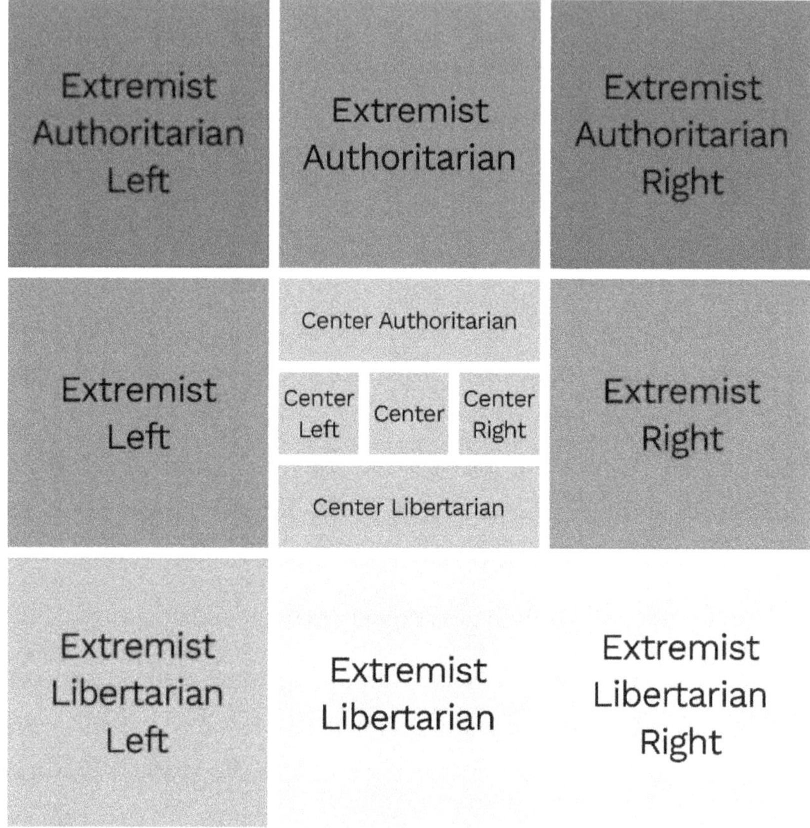

There are many criticisms leveled at centrism. For example, it is no more than a reflexive defense of the current status quo. At its worst, that is a genuine problem with this approach. But true centrism requires critical thinking to guard against these pitfalls. It is built on an active rejection of dogma coupled with a commitment to reasoned debate, the pursuit of cooperation, and the protection of the rights of all. Like all worthwhile causes, this approach is not easy to uphold, but it is well worth it.

This ideological compass has nine boxes to represent categories of ideology. It aims to represent all major categories of social ideologies. Only one of the nine boxes represents a non-extremist, balanced, or democratic approach: the centrist box.

This section of the compass contains all the ideologies that don't hold fanatical or extreme beliefs or views. Instead, it is home to fair, just, balanced views that benefit all and promote the well-being of society at large. Within this central area, you find generalist and particularist views, meaning left-wing and right-wing perspectives, as well as varying perceptions of concentrated and dispersed power. Only beyond this "centrist box" do you find ideologies classified as far-right, far-left, extremist right, or extremist left. Both "far" and "extremist" describe types of extremist ideologies. Similarly, along the vertical axis of the compass, views range from dispersed to concentrated power, with the north and south poles representing authoritarianism and libertarianism, respectively.

An individual may hold a particularist view of nationalism, prioritizing their nation and its national interests, and still be considered centrist. However, when they emphasize their race or ethnicity as the central component of politics because of superiority, they become too extreme to be considered part of the center. Similarly, a person may hold generalist views of socialism. But when they support taking away a person's right to property, as communists do, their beliefs become overly generalist and excessive. They violate a person's fundamental rights, and those who support these actions are extremists.

Democracy = Centrism

We have established that ideology is the fundamental element determining the type and makeup of a society. It has a decisive shaping influence on the government, economic systems, and culture. Now we examine the category in which liberal democratic republics and free nations belong.

Liberalism falls within the centrist category. That means, by extension, human rights and freedoms, democracy, republicanism, constitutionalism, free markets, and the entire American experiment do as well. So do all the functioning liberal democracies around the world. If you think about it carefully, a truly liberal democratic republic cannot be overly particularist or right-wing extremist. If it were, it would only prioritize specific individuals and groups while disadvantaging everyone else. In that case, the country would not be a true liberal democracy. Meanwhile, overly generalist or left-wing extremist positions are not compatible with liberalism either, as they would not sufficiently respect the rights of individuals.

Free-market capitalism is also, in essence, a centrist approach. Other forms of economic organization, such as feudalism, are not. In feudalism, a handful of nobles own land and take away people's rights based on their status at birth. Meanwhile, communism automatically guarantees everyone a share of everything, regardless of their contribution. That approach strips away any connection between effort and reward. Capitalism, at its best, tries to balance opportunity: you don't start with everything or nothing - it's what you do that counts. It is a system in which each and every individual in society has the right and the opportunity, regardless of race, ethnicity, gender, or background, to acquire land, resources, and the many other benefits that a man or woman rightfully earns through his or her talent and hard work. However, at the same time, it provides a welfare system - a social safety net - from which the less fortunate in society can benefit.

The decentralizing power of capitalism, combined with the limited government power and control over the economy, creates a perfect balance. People have the ability to acquire private property and capital, to build infrastructure, and to trade freely. At the same time, the government provides the necessary involvement through enforcing private-property laws, regulating industry where needed, using taxation wisely, and maintaining public order and stability. This balanced system gives people access to the resources they need while preserving the freedom to create, innovate, and trade. It also includes essential laws to protect consumers, the poor, and environmental interests.

In the end, this creates a perfect social environment with just enough freedom and just enough government involvement in the economy to inspire business leaders and investor confidence. It incentivizes them to invest and trade while still protecting the broader interests of society at large. It is this extraordinary system that generates the massive technological advancement and innovation, as well as the massive wealth, seen only in centrist societies.

If done right and in moderation - without redistributing excessive amounts of wealth from those who generate value to the less fortunate - the system works for everyone. Any time this redistribution is done, whether in excess or even in moderation, it almost always causes economic value to disappear. When wealth is redistributed in such a way, there is usually no economic return in wealth or value, so that value simply vanishes from the economy. It also de-incentivizes value generators from working or creating more, because the higher the percentage of a person's earnings that is taken, the less incentive they have to continue producing. However, when the necessary monetary assistance is provided for welfare and social programs that help the less fortunate or Americans who have fallen on hard times, the system benefits all of society. It becomes the only system capable of generating enough value to meet the needs of the less fortunate.

Today the system is out of balance. On the right, extremists want a laissez-faire capitalism - a system that benefits only the wealthy and provides little or no social safety net or welfare for the millions of Americans who rely on it. This is seen in Republican-controlled states like Texas, where massive wealth gaps exist between the rich and the poor. On the other hand, extremists on the left want an excessively socialist economic policy in which massive amounts of wealth are unproductively redistributed. This removes the incentive for value generators to create wealth and causes large amounts of economic value to disappear from society, creating economic inefficiencies, inflation, and decline. This is seen in excessively socialist states like California and New York, where poverty and the reduced well-being of disadvantaged communities have persisted for years with very little positive change.

The health of democracy depends on its centrism. It does not overly prioritize a single individual or group that traditionally held power in society. At the same time, it is not excessively generalist. Democracy, at least in its best liberal form, does not rob individuals of the rightful reward of their labor, unlike the communist system, which organizes humanity like a herd whose entire identity is tied to their class or the state. It recognizes that the beauty of humanity lies in our human individualism, expressed uniquely in our talents, abilities, and character. That differentiation means that when we unite as a society, we become indispensable pieces in a system of trade that has produced massive wealth and technological advancement. That is why liberal democratic nations, which remain true to their centrist orientation, are often made up of enlightened people, empowered in character and identity. Their citizens stand among the most empowered women and respected men in the world.

Whether in economics, politics, or anything else, the success of centrism cannot be denied. Whether through technological innovation, wealth not only for a select few but for all in society (if done right), or political efficiency, history has shown that the closer a given society is aligned with the ideals of centrism, the greater its success will be.

Extremism: the Synonym of Evil

The danger of extremism is very real. There are countless historical examples of the evils committed by extremist groups. The Nazis in Germany are a prime example. They sought the extermination of Jews based on an unsubstantiated racist doctrine. They blamed Jews for Germany's misfortunes, while paradoxically claiming they were inferior despite the substantial influence they allegedly wielded. To square this circle, Nazi ideology labeled Jews as a disease, a corrupting influence on society, and spread unfounded conspiracy theories about them. This ideology inspired a brutal extermination campaign. The Nazis pursued this vile goal with unprecedented brutality. In the concentration and death camps they built, unimaginable atrocities were committed: experiments on children, torture, rape, forced labor, and starvation. My words do not even begin to describe the true scale of the horror committed.

Meanwhile, the Soviet Union, which President Reagan accurately labeled as the "evil empire," was another regime that was responsible for the violation of human rights on a massive scale. They stripped away fundamental freedoms, including free speech and property rights, diminishing the minds and spirits of the people they claimed to represent. These abuses aimed to reduce their citizens to mindless, enslaved people who relied on the state to think for them, completely lacking any individuality or richness of character that citizens of free nations enjoy. Those who dared to challenge the regime faced brutal consequences, including imprisonment, death, torture, and exile to Siberia. The Soviets also committed wartime atrocities during World War II on a vast scale. It was the communist Soviets who were responsible for the largest mass rape in history. Hundreds of thousands of innocent civilian women and girls in Soviet-occupied territories were sexually assaulted; in many cases, these were gang rapes. These crimes occurred not only in enemy territories such as Germany (which is still a crime, as most civilian women and children were innocent), but even in supposedly friendly territories such as Poland. All told, the Soviet regime left an enduring mark of trauma and terror.

In more modern times, extremist Jihadist groups have become the central fulcrum of terrorism in the world, committing infamous atrocities like 9/11. It is worth noting that the Jihadist approach does not represent all of Islam. Instead, it can be classified as an extremist group within Islam. These extremist groups have brought terrorism to new levels of destruction by using modern technology to achieve fanatical religious goals.

Their tactics are cruel but also deeply cowardly. They use civilians, women, and children as human shields. They often put hospitals, schools, and daycare centers in danger by using them as bases of operation. They do this because they know many of their enemies - like the United States, Britain, and other liberal democracies - possess a sense of morality and generally abide by humanitarian international law. To be sure, these nations have also committed crimes on occasion, such as the My Lai massacre or several massacres committed by the British as part of their colonial rule. But those responsible have often faced charges, and in many cases, apologies and reparations have been offered. In other words, liberal democracies possess a sense of decency, unlike the terrorists.

Jihadist ideology also oppresses and strips women of their fundamental rights. Look no further than the treatment of women in countries like Iran to see the consequences of this ideology in action. Jihadist extremist groups have been responsible for heinous crimes, including the systematic sexual violence and rape of women and girls. These acts are so horrific that they challenge our very sense of humanity. How can we still call "human" those who stoop to such depravity - who celebrate atrocities as vile as the gang rape of a child?

We have firmly established that extremism is associated with atrocities. However, it is not just the moral depravity involved that poses a threat to society, but also that many of their systems - political, economic, and otherwise - tend to fail to achieve success.

Consider, for example, two of the most extreme ideologies: feudalism, which is right-wing, and communism, which is left-wing. In the feudal system, land and resources were controlled by an elite hierarchy. At the top stood a monarch who granted large estates to nobles, who in turn entrusted parts of the land to vassals. These lords oversaw peasants or serfs who performed long, hard labor. Power and wealth were concentrated among this select ruling class, while the vast majority of the population lived under strict obligations and limited freedoms.

This system deprived countless talented, hard-working individuals of access to the necessary land, resources, and infrastructure needed for innovation, creativity, and technological advancement. For that reason, feudal societies were consistently deprived of the massive prosperity that a free society can offer. This system also lacked patriotism and national loyalty and was therefore more prone to rebellion, as people tend to overthrow systems that do not genuinely benefit them or advance their interests.

The weaknesses of communism include a lack of national patriotism, the emigration of citizens to freer societies, and numerous other systemic flaws. One of the most significant problems, however, is economic inefficiency. In a communist system, the government centralizes economic management and decision-making. History has shown that this leads to a range of inefficiencies, such as producing goods for which there is little or no demand while failing to produce goods that are actually needed. This results in vast amounts of resources being spent with little or no return. As more and more resources and wealth are poured into areas in which there is no economic return, society's economic value and resources eventually run low, destabilizing the system. Importantly, this represents only one of many inefficiencies inherent in the system; taken together, these inefficiencies compound over time and ultimately lead to economic stagnation and widespread poverty, or, in some cases - as seen with the Soviet Union's economy - collapse.

I have only scratched the surface in describing what extremism can do to a society. There are a plethora of other groups and ideologies that could be named, each leaving a trail of suffering and destruction in its wake. The horrific acts committed in the name of extremist beliefs are a stain on humanity, reminding us of the depths to which we can fall when driven by blind fanaticism.

CHAPTER 2:

Extremism in America

Extremists attack a society like a plague. It degrades everything it touches. In America, the plague infected our political system. That has led to the polarity and unprecedented political chaos and dysfunction evident today. Among the results are the destruction of police stations, rioting, storming of government buildings, and political assassinations. Make no mistake: it is no coincidence that the era marked by rising prices, economic insecurity, and escalating political and social unrest has also been the era in which extremism on both the left and the right has gained strength in American politics

America has faced many forms of extremism, including extremist far-left, extremist far-right, religious, authoritarian, and others throughout its history. This chapter will cover some of the more dangerous extremist ideologies that have some of the most prominent types of anti-American-Extremist ideas that have gained influence in American society.

The massive political polarization we see today is essentially the product of two relatively small groups of warring factions on the right and left that have taken over the Republican and Democratic parties, respectively. These extremists succeeded in eliminating opposition, including more moderate views or options. The same repressive ideas that are behind the worst totalitarian movements in the world are now informing much of the leadership of the Republican and Democratic parties.

Both sides resorted to drastic measures to hold on to power. They are not above breaking the law and engaging in violence. Support for attacks on law enforcement has increased. Therefore, there is also an increase in vandalism and rioting. The storming of the Capitol Building was a case in point. Government buildings. There are ideological reasons for this. Extremist philosophers like Karl Marx are admired by many, and it is no longer taboo to speak highly of authoritarian leaders like Xi Jinping and Vladimir Putin. Meanwhile, others support naming U.S. military bases after Confederate generals, even though known for their racism.

These are the reasons that we have seen increasing division in American politics. However, America is not nearly as divided as it seems. Data consistently show that most Americans can agree on most political and social issues. That is because more than half of the American electorate identifies as moderate or centrist. Indeed, most Americans reject the extremist views and positions that many political leaders on the left and right have taken. The American people are not responsible for the country's growing polarization. Instead, it is a small number of warring extremist factions on both sides that cause the problem. This means we can rid the system of much of the extremism. Without it, we could be much stronger and more united as a nation.

But these Extremists have the momentum. They are achieving their goal of hijacking the electoral process, making it essentially impossible for third options or ideas to gain traction. The next step for each of these warring factions' goals is to eliminate the other and take complete control of our nation.

Economic Results of Extremism

There are economic consequences to this troubling situation. Millions of Americans find they are unable to enjoy the wealth and prosperity enjoyed by previous generations. The cost of living is out of control. Every dollar earned is worth far less today than it was in the past. The cost of necessities has robbed millions of Americans of the American dream. Inflation has steadily been increasing in the United States for decades. At the time of writing, the annual inflation rate has been 4.18%. You have to pay a lot more for necessities like gas and groceries, sometimes as much as double.

But what is the cause of this problem? Inflation is not a complex concept. It is one of the first things taught in high school economics. You might remember a teacher telling you that inflation is just what happens when there is too much money in circulation in relation to available goods and services. The more money you have in circulation, the more prices will rise.

Because inflation is caused by too much money in circulation, the entity responsible is the one printing too much money. Everything else news anchors and government officials talk about endlessly to distract the American public at large from that leading cause is a mere distraction.

To be sure, the government does not deliberately print excess money to cause inflation. It does so because it is forced to, as the U.S. government runs massive deficits, and printing additional cash is a way to pay for them. This causes prices across the market to rise, forcing the American public to pay higher prices. In other words, you, the American citizen, are paying for unnecessary government spending. Even marginal price increases are usually correlated with increases in the governmental deficit.

On an ideological level, policies involving massive government spending and deficits often feed off the idea that the government is the engine of wealth and economic growth. In this view, the private sector, the American worker, and entrepreneurs play a less critical role. This ideological approach encourages elected officials to spend far too much, believing there will not be adverse consequences to contend with. It is a frame of mind inspired by Socialist and Communist ideals. In America, this approach has been expressed in the "woke" mindset.

These policies have had adverse consequences on many American cities. You could be one of the millions of Americans who leave deep-blue states like California, New York, and Illinois for these reasons. These states have experienced economic decline due to the harmful "woke" agenda. California and New York once led the American economy. Now they are better known for slow growth and inefficiency. The innovation they once excelled at has stalled as the local economy staggers under the weight of overregulation and high taxes. Therefore, California has experienced an increase in unemployment. Jobs in the private sector declined by a massive 46,000 since January 2023 (San Francisco Chronicle, 2025). California has experienced significant slowdowns in GDP growth, and jobs in the private sector have declined by a massive 46,000 since January 2023.

The economic ideology these state leaders have adopted comes from the same roots as that adopted by the Soviet Union, North Korea, Cuba, and China before they liberalized their economies. Their leadership seems to believe that despite the severe economic collapse of the Soviet Union, China's struggle to feed its own citizens before embracing free-market reforms, the stark divide between North Korea's extreme poverty and South Korea's booming economy, and the mass exodus of hundreds of thousands of Cubans fleeing Communist Cuba for the freedom and prosperity of Florida, perhaps this time will be different. That is the only reasonable conclusion or argument any person who still believes in this ideology can make. They think that maybe if New York, California, and Illinois adopt a more socialist economic policy, they can stop the mass exodus of their citizens leaving those states and fix their mounting financial problems if they could only double down on their socialism.

The data is unequivocal. The areas of the United States that are Democrat controlled and have Woke-Socialist economic policy experience a decline of financial security, an increase in homelessness, a mass exodus of businesses and citizens, debt, infrastructure problems, and a litany of other economic inefficiencies. Florida and Texas are the beneficiaries of the economic decline of blue states. Their GDP has grown, mainly thanks to the bolstered technology sector. These states have become the new hub for business activity in the United States.

Economically Sound Wealth Generators But Only for a SELECT FEW

These trends have benefited Republican-led states like Florida and Texas. Voters tend to view Republicans as better on the economy than Democrats. However, even though Republicans and those on the far-right that have become the majority within the Republican party (although there are still some that aren't as extremist within it) are economically more sound and competent, they usually favor or prioritize certain classes within society. Even though these states generate massive amounts of wealth, too few people fully receive its benefits.

Therefore, the benefits of their economic policy extend only to the upper middle class, with fewer benefits for the rest of the middle class. The lower middle class and below are left out. Project 2025 is an example of the way the extreme right wing encourages inequality. The approach calls to cut funding for social and welfare programs. Ignoring the plight of the millions who depend on them for survival.

These heartless policies are being implemented right now. Single parents and people with disabilities are particularly at risk. Meanwhile, the increasingly large number of Americans living in poverty who depend on Medicaid, SNAP (Food Stamps), school meals, and child nutrition programs, such as Head Start, are in danger of losing support. The plans of Project 2025 place over 800,000 low-income children at risk of losing essential services. Access to education services, TANF (Temporary Assistance for Needy Families), public housing, and other social safety-net programs is under threat. The agenda is clear. The destruction of the American social welfare system, so that the economic consists of pure laissez-faire capitalism.

Supposedly, these cuts are designed to alleviate the national debt. However, Project 2025 is massively expensive. It just reallocates the money to extreme interests, instead of providing it to the needy.

Attack on Free Speech

There is a growing assault on free speech. It is derived from an impulse to shut down alternatives to the two big parties. Limiting debate helps them maintain their monopoly. I find the woke attack on free speech deeply shocking. It has been pursued with appalling openness. While some opponents of free speech hide their goals, the woke movement has been unapologetic in its suppression.

Some senior leaders in the Democrat party have gone so far as to attack the First Amendment directly, calling it an "obstacle" and "an enabler of extremism." The irony is that this stance is itself clearly extreme. They call the Constitution "an enabler of extremism" because of its defense of free speech, yet the person who attacks human rights (which free speech is) holds a classic belief of an extremist: the suppression of human rights.

During the 2024 election, Meta CEO Mark Zuckerberg publicly revealed how the Biden administration pressured Facebook to censor free speech. The government repeatedly threatened social media companies in an effort to censor information about the COVID-19 pandemic and other hot topics. Most alarmingly, much of the material they wanted removed was factually accurate. However, it threatened the "woke" agenda. The problem goes far beyond the Biden administration. The "woke" movement and its leaders have often sought to censor information on social media.

The problem is even more acute in Europe. There, the forces of "wokeness" routinely pass laws violating freedom of speech. It has almost reached the level of making specific thoughts illegal. The United Kingdom seems particularly far gone. It has passed several laws, such as the Malicious Communications Act 1988, rendering particular forms of speech illegal.

Meanwhile, Brazil faces challenges to free speech. The country once enjoyed a reputation for democratic progress. But that has changed. Supreme Court justice Alexandre de Moraes has investigated politicians and limiting freedom of speech, while claiming to oppose disinformation. The prosecution of former President Jair Bolsonaro, has been a particular concern.

When free speech is attacked, other human rights violations often accompany it. This is not a coincidence. The result is increased government involvement in individuals' lives, and that road leads to authoritarianism.

No government has the right to tell a full-grown adult how to think or what to say. Individuals enjoy rights and liberties to protect them from that. The liberal democratic system of government is founded on the right to free speech. Citizens should enjoy the absolute right to say, think, and feel whatever they want. The only limitation is when the rights of others are infringed.

Freedom of speech and human equality go hand-in-hand. If someone believes a government official can control what others say or think, they're saying one opinion is superior to another. In effect, this ideology makes government officials masters of others' thoughts and minds. Why would a self-respecting person reduce themselves to that? And make no mistake, elected officials may think they are superior to the citizens, but they are not.

Their role is not to serve as masters, but rather to serve the public. A government should protect life, liberty, and property. They do not have the right to enforce interpretations of morality at our expense.

Violence of Extremism

Political extremism in the United States has repeatedly erupted into violence, leaving communities scarred, families shattered, and public institutions under threat. While the vast majority of Americans engage in politics peacefully, a small but dangerous minority has repeatedly turned to violence to advance extremist goals. These acts, whether carried out by left-wing or right-wing extremists, strike at democracy, public safety, and the very social fabric of the nation. Each incident leaves behind a trail of trauma, fear, and loss that reverberates far beyond the immediate victims, touching entire communities and institutions.

Right-wing extremist violence has left some of the deepest and most widely known scars. On January 6, 2021, the U.S. Capitol was violently breached by thousands seeking to overturn the 2020 presidential election. Inside, officers struggled against an onslaught of bodies, shields, and makeshift weapons. Ashli Babbitt, a 35-year-old Air Force veteran, was fatally shot as she attempted to climb through a breached window, while Officer Brian Sicknick later died after injuries sustained during the attack.

The chaos inside the Capitol was overwhelming. Officers scrambled to defend both themselves and lawmakers, who were trapped in offices as rioters surged through the halls. Windows were smashed, furniture overturned, and makeshift weapons swung at those trying to maintain order. Officers reported feeling surrounded and outnumbered, while staffers cowered under desks, clutching one another in fear. The sounds of shouting, breaking glass, and sudden gunfire created an environment where seconds felt like hours, leaving many with lasting trauma long after the event.

Families watching from home described helplessness, disbelief, and fear for the lives of those inside, a vivid reminder that political extremism can transform everyday spaces into sites of terror.

Other right-wing attacks highlight the devastating personal toll of extremism. On October 27, 2018, the Tree of Life synagogue in Pittsburgh became the site of the deadliest antisemitic attack in U.S. history. Eleven congregants were murdered, including Joyce Fienberg, 75; Richard Gottfried, 65; Rose Mallinger, 97; Jerry Rabinowitz, 66; Cecil and David Rosenthal, 59 and 54; Bernice and Sylvan Simon, 84 and 86; Daniel Stein, 71; Melvin Wax, 87; and Irving Younger, 69.

The scene was one of sheer panic and confusion. Congregants initially mistook the first gunshots for objects falling, a routine sound in the bustling synagogue. But then the horror became undeniable. Survivors described the gunman moving methodically through the sanctuary, shooting congregants at close range. One man shielded his granddaughter beneath a pew, both trembling as bullets tore through the room. Others threw themselves over loved ones, trying to stop them from being struck. The cries of the wounded, mixed with the sounds of gunfire, created an atmosphere of unrelenting terror. Survivors spoke later of the physical and psychological scars: permanent anxiety, nightmares, and the haunting replay of the screams they could not silence.

In June 2015, Dylann Roof entered the Emanuel African Methodist Episcopal Church in Charleston, South Carolina, during Bible study and opened fire, killing nine African American worshippers. The victims were cherished family members, friends, and community leaders, including Clementa Pinckney, the church's pastor and a state senator. Survivors described the horror of ducking for cover as bullets tore through the church, the crushing sorrow of realizing loved ones had been murdered in a place meant for refuge.

The experience of the survivors was terrifyingly intimate. One woman shielded her niece beneath a pew, feeling the vibrations of each bullet strike nearby. Another tried to crawl toward a doorway but was stopped by the fallen body of a neighbor, forcing her to change direction while the sound of gunfire echoed off the walls. The trauma was compounded by the knowledge that the attacker showed no remorse. Roof wrote in a jailhouse journal, "I would like to make it crystal clear I do not regret what I did. I am not sorry. I have not shed a tear for the innocent people I killed." He framed the killings as an ideological mission, expressing sympathy only for what he saw as "innocent white children...forced to live in this sick country." During his trial, he reiterated that he had nothing wrong with him psychologically and did not seek mercy, a chilling reminder of the calculated, deliberate nature of such violence.

These incidents illustrate that right-wing extremist attacks are often not only lethal but deeply personal and psychologically devastating. Victims' experiences encompass moments of acute terror, the scramble for survival, and the haunting aftermath that extends well beyond the physical injuries. Families, friends, and communities are left to grapple with grief and the lasting effects of trauma while society as a whole witnesses the erosion of a sense of safety and the violation of spaces meant to provide refuge and civic stability.

Left-wing extremist violence has also produced incidents of shocking and sudden brutality. In September 2025, Charlie Kirk, a prominent conservative activist, was assassinated at a public speaking event in Utah. What began as a routine appearance turned into a tragedy. As Kirk stepped to the podium, the room buzzing with applause, a single gunshot cracked through the hall. For a moment, attendees froze, mistaking the sound for a dropped microphone. Then horror erupted.

Bodies hit the floor as people scrambled for cover. Kirk was struck multiple times before security could react. Paramedics worked frantically, navigating the panic-stricken crowd to reach him. Friends, colleagues, and strangers alike were left in disbelief. Vigils spontaneously emerged across towns and cities, with citizens lighting candles, not only for Kirk, but for the fragile idea that political violence could suddenly shatter ordinary life.

For Kirk's family, the loss was unimaginable. His partner and children had spent months preparing for the event, unaware that it would culminate in such irreversible tragedy. His brother recalled Kirk's last words, not political rhetoric, but a story meant to make his children laugh - words that would never again be heard. In that instant, the nation saw how political extremism could turn ordinary civic life into a scene of grief and trauma.

Earlier that summer, in July 2025, a group of left-wing extremists targeted a U.S. Immigration and Customs Enforcement detention facility in Alvarado, Texas. The attackers deployed fireworks to create confusion and obscured visibility, then opened fire on responding officers. Officer Miguel Alvarez, a 12-year veteran of the local force, was struck in the neck and fell, his partner at his side calling for help amid the chaos. Other officers ducked behind barriers as bullets cracked the air, smoke from fireworks filling the night.

Inside the facility, detainees and staff huddled, uncertain if the gunfire would escalate into a full breach. Some pressed themselves under desks; others whispered prayers in fear. Outside, neighbors who had been celebrating Independence Day were suddenly confronted with explosions and gunfire, the familiar safety of their streets shattered. Alvarez survived, but the nights of anxiety and startle reactions would linger, a permanent reminder of the day ideology turned violent.

Earlier violence that year had already demonstrated how extremism can cause fear even without fatalities. In March 2023, an anarchist group set fire to a federal courthouse in Philadelphia while law enforcement officers were present. Flames erupted unexpectedly, sending thick smoke into hallways where judges, clerks, and officers were working. Two officers were injured by burns and smoke inhalation. Evacuations were chaotic, with people stumbling through smoke-filled corridors, clinging to one another in fear. The courthouse itself suffered structural damage, displacing essential government operations for weeks and leaving a community to confront the reality that even spaces representing justice are vulnerable to deliberate attack.

Property destruction and arson have also marked left-wing extremist actions in Portland, Oregon, and Seattle, Washington. One night in downtown Portland began as a protest march, voices raised, banners waving, before escalating into violent chaos. Storefront windows were shattered, trash cans set ablaze, and smoke reflected in the city's neon lights. Business owners like Tasha Nguyen watched years of labor reduced to rubble, clutching mementos of their achievements as flames licked the streets. Residents and families were caught in the turmoil, rerouted from home, ducking projectiles, and facing the visceral, unpredictable danger of ideologically driven unrest. Even after the fires were extinguished, the psychological aftermath remained, etching fear and unease into the community's collective memory.

Across both right- and left-wing extremism, patterns of brutality emerge. Extremists often target symbols of authority, ideology, or communal identity: government buildings, detention centers, law enforcement, religious institutions, and public gatherings. Violence can escalate from property damage to mass shootings and assassinations, demonstrating the full spectrum of risk. The human toll is profound: survivors endure physical injuries, emotional trauma, and a lasting sense of vulnerability. Communities experience collective fear, uncertainty, and erosion of trust in institutions designed to protect them. Each attack leaves ripples far beyond the immediate scene, affecting civic participation, neighborhood safety, and national perception of stability.

The recent history of political violence in the United States offers a sobering lesson: extremism, regardless of ideology, is a direct and immediate threat to life and democracy. The Capitol riot, the Charleston church shooting, and the Pittsburgh synagogue attack, alongside the assassination of Charlie Kirk, the Alvarado ICE facility ambush, the Philadelphia courthouse arson, property destruction in major cities, and many other examples of extremist violence, reveal the human cost of radicalization. Lives are lost, families are devastated, neighborhoods traumatized, and public trust eroded. Political extremism is not a theoretical danger; it is a brutal, tangible threat.

The first Casualty of War is Truth, but not in a Just War.

The war between left and right-wing extremists is dirty and desperate. The two sides are so intent on winning and destroying the other that they resort to manipulating and deceiving the American people. Politicians to media on both sides of the aisle, twist the truth. Even tragedies are downplayed when they don't fit the preferred narrative. The right tried to ignore the death of George Floyd, and the left-wing media did not report the gruesome death of Iryna Zarutska, because those cases were inconvenient to their narrative.

Right-wing news outlets like Fox News downplayed or refused to cover the mention of Donald Trump's name in the Epstein Files and his shady business deals - while left-wing outlets not only covered it but dramatized it. Conversely, left-leaning outlets covered little of the Biden family's possible corruption and business dealings in places like Ukraine, while right-wing media amplified it.

During the COVID-19 pandemic, right-wing figures and media frequently minimized the severity of the virus, questioned death counts, and framed public-health measures as purely authoritarian overreach, even when hospitals were overwhelmed. At the same time, left-leaning politicians and media overstated certainty around evolving science, dismissed legitimate questions as misinformation, and downplayed the social and economic harm caused by prolonged lockdowns and school closures.

Narrative manipulation is also evident in how protests and violence are portrayed. When riots followed protests aligned with left-wing causes, many left-leaning outlets framed the events as "mostly peaceful," minimizing property destruction and attacks on civilians. When violence occurred at right-wing events - most notably January 6 - right-wing media often shifted focus away from the conduct itself and toward broader grievances, portraying participants as patriots or victims of provocation rather than addressing the severity of their actions.

Foreign policy offers another clear example. The withdrawal from Afghanistan was initially portrayed by many left-leaning outlets as an unavoidable logistical challenge, downplaying intelligence failures and the human cost to Afghan allies. Right-wing media later weaponized the chaos, presenting it as proof of total incompetence while ignoring similar failures under prior administrations. Each side emphasized blame while avoiding honest accountability.

Economic reporting follows the same pattern. When inflation surged during the Biden administration, left-leaning outlets attributed it almost exclusively to global forces and corporate greed, minimizing the role of domestic policy decisions. Right-leaning media framed inflation as entirely self-inflicted by the administration in power, often ignoring broader post-pandemic economic conditions. Neither side presented a complete picture.

Even language itself is manipulated. Terms like "insurrection," "threat to democracy," "fascism," and "socialism" are routinely stretched beyond their precise meanings to provoke fear and loyalty. Complex policy disagreements are reduced to moral absolutes, ensuring that compromise appears as betrayal rather than governance.

Whether they twist the truth or outright lie, in the end the truth is always manipulated in some form. In each case, the tactic is the same: emphasize what helps, suppress what harms, and present interpretation as fact. The manipulation is rarely subtle - and it is rarely one-sided.

You may have heard the saying that one of the first casualties of war is truth. As domestic politics have become a battlefield, that is now the sad truth.

However, if this were a just political war, truth would be the victor. Unfortunately, that is not the case. Both sides prefer to twist the truth and claim that the other is going against the Constitution. But they both have turned their backs on liberal-democratic principles. They increasingly ignore the law when convenient. Therefore, they are mirror images of extremism.

In their battle for supremacy, the extremists are lying to you and trying to manipulate you. When you turn on the news, listen to politicians and activists speak, you are listening to the products of a right-wing and left-wing extremist propaganda machine used to wage one of the biggest social wars in history. To be sure, there are exceptions. Not all politicians, activists, reporters, and anchors are engaged in this process. Unfortunately, the moderate voices are an ever-dwindling minority on the airwaves.

Ambiguity in Condemnation

Many on the right, most notably Mr. Trump, refuse to condemn extremist historical figures. The veneration of Confederate generals is a primary example. Chris Wallace asked the President, "Is the Confederate flag offensive?" Trump's response was, "It depends on who you're talking about when you're talking about." Trump said that it is not a symbol of slavery but rather embodies southern heritage. In another case, the President was asked about it, and pivoted by saying, "It's freedom of speech, you do what you do, it's freedom of speech."

The administration has also defended the statues of Confederate generals and leaders. They restored the names of Military bases named after Confederate generals, after their predecessors had changed them. To cover this move, Trump officials pretended it was now named after other leaders of the same name. How convenient.

Many Republicans are more than happy to wholeheartedly and emphatically condemn any hint of extremism if it is on the left. Rightfully so. But when it comes to right-wing forms of extremism, they refuse to do the same and instead take confusingly ambiguous stances. Like saying that it is "freedom of speech" or "a person has a right to their own views." This is a hypocritical double standard. They would wholeheartedly condemn somebody waving a communist flag, but when it's a Confederate flag, it becomes free speech.

Republican hypocrisy raises uncomfortable questions. Do they truly admire the slave owning Confederacy? If so, can they be trusted to uphold democratic ideals like equality?

The right responds to these questions evasively. Answers such as these: "It's hard to define right-wing extremism," "Is that really extreme?" "People have a right to feel how they want," or "It's not my place to judge," avoid confronting the issue. However, the right is never ambiguous when confronting left-wing extremism. The left is the same way. They will condemn extremism on the other side, while ignoring their own.

Attack on the Innocent

Having ideas that are fanatical and antithetical to human rights, such as sexism and racism, is bad enough. But it is far worse when your ideals harm the most innocent people in society, when you use your power to take advantage of the weak, and when you prey on children. Those who do so reduce themselves to the lowest and most vile amongst humanity. By doing so, they become the number one enemy of society. Child predators are the most dangerous criminals and commit the most horrific crimes against humanity.

What if I told you that a specific law had been passed that would make it possible for your child to verbally consent to having some form of sexual interaction with an adult, and they could do so? Meanwhile, if you tried to intervene and protect your child, you could face legal consequences.

This is not a theoretical situation. California passed the AB 1955 bill, which would allow school teachers to approve sex change procedures for children in secrecy without notifying their parents. These measures would include hormone blockers, sex change surgeries - such as invasive and irreversible procedures like vaginoplasty (reshaping the penis into a vagina) - and other treatments that alter sexual organs and hormone levels. Furthermore, at the state's discretion, this bill would even give the state the power to take children away from their parents if the state tries to intervene. This constitutes a clear and blatant violation of parental rights.

This law does three disgusting things: it violates parents' rights, legalizes kidnapping, and facilitates sexual interaction with minors. It is well-established that minors are incapable of consenting or making decisions regarding adult matters such as sex. That is what it means when an adult performs a procedure to manipulate their sexual organs through surgery or their hormones.

Allowing a minor to consent to sex change procedures and surgeries can be compared to giving them the ability to decide whether to engage in sexual activity with an adult. It leaves them vulnerable to manipulation and grooming.

Regardless of their failed economics, reverse prejudice, reverse sexism, and reverse racism, this alone would render the woke ideology one of the most extreme and evil ideologies in human history. Many ideologies allowed for the violation of human rights and encouraged racist and sexist views. However, few so openly hold views that facilitate the exploitation of the vulnerability of children as the woke ideology does.

If someone supports an ideology that condones harming children and performing invasive, irreversible bodily sexual tampering on little boys and girls, that person is a danger to society and humanity. It has no business being in positions of power.

What is Woke?

What is Woke? It was supposed to be an ideology designed to wake people up to social injustice. The goal was to alert people to the oppression many experience in society through the scourges of racism, sexism, and extremism. I do not doubt that there were good, honest people who were proponents of that philosophy, especially in its early stages. Even today, some in that camp truly wish to fight against injustice and are devoid of fanaticism.

One such person is well-known podcaster and influencer Amala Ekpunobi. She has often said she honestly believed she was on the side of justice when she was a woke activist. It was only later that she saw the ideology behind it was actually extremist.

Unfortunately, there are millions of Americans and people in other Western countries who are ignorant of the true nature of the woke ideology. They have been infected with what one of the world's leading technology entrepreneurs, Elon Musk, frequently calls the "Woke mind virus." I only hope that they are not so far gone that they can't recover.

Despite the good intentions behind the woke movement, those involved have tarnished it. It has become the very thing it was intended to fight against. Woke has become the ideology of racism, sexism, injustice, and extremism. A Nazi inspired by Hitler's ideology is as evil as a Communist driven by Marxist-Stalinist beliefs, just as a white supremacist is as bigoted as someone who embraces reverse racism as a result of their wokeness.

The Republican Party: The Party that Defends Individual Rights and Freedoms?

With the Democrat party being overtaken by woke extremists, some believe that the Republican Party is now the defender of liberty and American individualism.

But if we are being honest, the extent to which the Republican Party defends human rights and freedoms is similar to the approach of the Democrats. In other words, they will only protect them when it suits their ideology.

A good example is legislation that many Republicans have supported that would severely limit or ban sexually explicit internet content. Whether the use of these services is morally right or wrong is not relevant to the fact that this legislation infringes on an individual's personal freedom regarding an issue that does not concern the state. Many activities raise moral questions and carry risks to health or well-being. For example, alcohol, cigarettes, high-risk sports, and hunting all involve potential harm and ethical concerns.

Oral questions can be raised, and individual health or well-being can be at risk. But since these habits affect only an individual, it is a personal decision, and the freedom to pursue them constitutes a human right. The government has no right or authority to police individuals in this regard. A fully grown adult must reckon with the consequences of their actions, as in every field of life. This kind of legislation runs counter to the purpose of a liberal democracy. That is a secular society in which the government protects rights and freedoms. It does not morally police its citizens. The responsibility of a liberal and democratic state is to defend life, liberty, and property, not act as a nanny to fully grown adult humans.

Another area of Republican hypocrisy pertains to one of the most hotly debated political topics. It is so complicated that some of the most significant political thinkers and social scientists have been unable to answer it: Does a woman have a right to an abortion?

The problem with the position many (but not all) on the right have taken is that they condemn abortion completely in all cases. They do this without stopping to think or analyze this complex issue. It involves balancing the rights of two individuals - the health and well-being of a woman, and the life of a child who, contrary to popular belief, is alive from the moment of conception.

So let's break this down and see if we can answer the question in line with liberal democratic ideals. Does a woman have absolute authority over what goes on with her body? Each answer has far-reaching implications. According to liberal ideology (not the left-leaning Democratic stance, but rather the philosophy that inspired the founding of the United States), the answer would be that the individual has complete authority over their body. Therefore, women enjoy final say in matters concerning their bodies. Thus, no third party has the right to force a woman to use her body to sustain another's life any more than one person does.

This is about human rights, not morality. Whether it is morally right or wrong for a woman to remove another person from the property of her body is an entirely different subject. That is a concerning religious or philosophical debate, not a political one. Our social contract calls to leave personal morality and religious views aside. Interference with a woman's property of the body violates her human rights and autonomy.

Religious beliefs heavily influence anti-abortion campaigns. But we live in a democracy, not a theocracy. America protects religious rights but doesn't enforce religious law. But proponents of campaigns and projects like Project 2025 fail to recognize that they are restricting human rights. The proposals within this project, if implemented, would end the mail delivery of abortion pills, cut off funding for entities involved in abortion services, and appoint federal officials to enforce anti-abortion laws strictly. But the greatest threat to bodily-property rights is that it encourages states to go even further and ban these rights completely.

I would feel morally compelled to use my body and resources to maintain the life of another, but that is my personal decision. A woman's body is her property over which she has absolute authority.

Extremism Shackles the Human Spirit

Extremism restrains human potential, suffocates genius. The over regulation and relentless tightening grip over the economy by government from extremist-left policies chokes the groundbreaking ideas of the genius, the innovative solutions of the business leader, and stifles national prosperity.

The outdated ways and old traditions of the past that the extremist-right so desperately clings onto holds back progress and halts the artistic creativity achieved through diversity.

It is because creativity and art, manifests through openness and diversity, the achievements of the genius, relies on liberty, and success comes when people are empowered.

Contained within the human spirit is an immeasurable amount of passion-driven potential. But extremism enslaves, crushes the human spirit. We must remove the shackles of extremism and liberate the human soul, the soul of this nation once again. Because only when men and women are free, unshackled, able to relentlessly pursue what the universe destines for them without restraints, can their power be released. Only in a free society of centrism can human potential be realized, only in a place where liberty is protected and rights are guaranteed can the passions of the soul create miracles of dreams manifested.

CHAPTER 3:

A Nation of the People A Solution for the People

Democracy deserves and requires protection. Doing so requires a new concept of democracy, which safeguards it from extremists. This would be called a centrist ideological democracy, or a Ceidocracy. Practically speaking, a Ceidocratic regime is one where extremist participation in the political process is outlawed. We have already established that an extremist ideology promotes ideals that violate human rights and advance prejudice or intolerance.

Why is this needed? The greatest strength of democracy is the legal protection it provides for human rights, freedom, equality, justice, and fairness. That has allowed democratic nations to lift billions out of poverty, as their citizens enjoy unrivaled prosperity and a strong social safety net. Despite its flaws, democracy offers an unrivaled level of fairness and equality. Women and minority groups are better able to fight for their rights and freedoms under its protection. Free men and women can follow their dreams. Therefore, they possess fantastic potential. This advantage is why democratic nations often lead the way in technology and innovation.

Our democracy is under threat. As we have seen, ideologies incompatible with democracy are the greatest problem our society faces. Therefore, a significant presence of ideologies of this sort in a society can weaken it significantly. How can you expect anyone who holds ideals antithetical to democracy to uphold its values and support its institutions, much less to protect the constitution?

For example, most extremist ideals involve censoring speech. Individuals who believe in censoring ideas they dislike are unlikely to defend the principle of free speech. They are far more likely to exploit loopholes or weaknesses to violate this sacred human right. Meanwhile, those with racist views are not capable of creating a just society. It doesn't matter if their prejudices are of the left-wing or right-wing variety. Their efforts will shape an unjust country. After all, men who think women are inferior cannot promote women's rights.

A woman who thinks all men are misogynistic will probably not be an enthusiastic supporter of men's rights. Meanwhile, religious fanatics won't fight for freedom of religion, and so on. Trusting these types of people (extremists) to participate in the political process is not unlike asking a pedophile to babysit.

That approach does not work. But that is our situation. Leaders with anti-democratic beliefs have been in charge in America for years. That is why the United States and other democracies are so dysfunctional. We have put our trust in the wrong people, and have paid the price.

The Challenge of Extremism in Democracy

Democracy's openness makes it vulnerable. Every ideology can influence it, and that can distort its most essential principles. By accepting all inputs, democracy sometimes becomes distorted. As extremist ideals enter, they warp it in unfair ways. Soon, some votes carry more weight than others, and loopholes that allow discrimination and human rights violations are identified, widened, and exploited. That has been the case in America.

That does not mean that the American experiment has failed. But it does mean a way to fix the crack in the fabric of democracy, which is slowly weakening and eroding its foundation, is desperately needed. The solution of Ceidocracy is simple and powerful. It will protect and strengthen freedom, equality, and justice - and guard against threats to democracy and human rights. This solution is to do more than outlaw particular cases of extremism as we do now. Instead, we remove the problem entirely through the Constitution. Nothing less than the supreme document will do. The goal is to allow only non-extremist views to prevail.

Implementing and Enforcing Ceidocracy

The Ceidocratic system can only function properly if the legislation supports it. In particular, legislation which protects the system from extremism. The most critical component of that effort will be to keep individuals with extremist ideals from harming the democratic system through their participation.

Of course, laws alone mean nothing. If they are not enforced, few obey. For example, the laws of the universe are enforced by reality itself, the laws of physics by the forces of nature, and the laws of society by the executive power.

Obviously, you cannot enforce a law fairly or justly unless those enforcing it truly understand its importance and purpose. If you are going to implement a law, you need individuals who specialize in it and who understand it inside and out, its deepest principles and its fundamental nature.

Law enforcement is highly specialized. It is up to local police to enforce state and municipal laws. The FBI and the DEA are responsible for investigating specific federal crimes. The role of U.S. Marshals is to enforce federal court orders, while regulatory bodies oversee compliance in their purview.

Many agencies create specialized units to handle complex crimes. Examples include human trafficking and money laundering. The personnel in these units is trained to handle their domain and enforce relevant laws.

Extremism is no different. An agency specializing in ideology- and extremist-related crimes is needed to enforce these laws appropriately and justly. That is a critical component of a Ceidocratic form of government.

The agents employed in the proposed extremism enforcement agency would have a range of complex duties. They would include identifying extremist ideologies, individuals, and groups. Meanwhile, they would enforce the anti-extremist laws that would provide their mandate. Perhaps most importantly, they would stop extremists from running for political office. They would also limit the voter pool to those who do not hold extremist views. Finally, they would investigate serious extremist threats in society. In sum, these efforts would help prevent the overtake of the democratic system by rioters, terrorists, or organized extremist groups, as the Nazis did in the Weimar Republic.

The officers in this organization will be tasked with protecting freedom, human rights, and a fair, just, and equal society. They serve as the frontline defense for centrist ideals.

Of course, their powers would be limited by the system's checks and balances. They would act pursuant to Congressional legislation, and the judiciary would interpret their authority.

The entire system would need to accommodate this effort. The judiciary will require training to interpret the new laws. But when the necessary adjustments are made, lawyers, judges, justices will be able to address questions of ideology and extremism successfully.

Categories of Extremists

There would be two categories of extremist: active and non-active. A non-active extremist is an individual who holds extremist ideals but is not actively pursuing them, either due to fear of legal punishment or because they believe achieving their goals is unlikely. This type of extremist would be prohibited from participating in the political process, as they cannot be trusted - similar to how a pedophile cannot be trusted in jobs, professions, or other roles involving children.

The other category is the active extremist. These are extremists who are actively attempting to implement their illegal ideals. These are dangerous people. They are capable, and even likely, to manipulate the democratic process to promote their ideological beliefs. Active extremists often engage in vandalism, terrorism, and even foment civil war.

This category is a much higher priority, as these individuals pose a greater threat to a democratic society. These individuals would also not be allowed to vote or stand for office. But they will also face legal ramifications for their actions. In some cases incarceration, or even more serious penalties if necessary.

The Power of Ceidocracy

Just think about the power a Ceidocratic form of government would have. The system prevents extremist laws from being passed, by keeping those who would pass them out of the system. By ensuring that extremist laws are no longer passed, the government can protect the political system and guarantee the protection of human rights.

Unfortunately, we are far from enjoying that security today. There is currently no law banning extremism in general. Instead, laws prohibit specific extremist actions or incitement to violence. For that reason, sometimes many years of human suffering pass, as rights abuses and violations accrue before action is taken. Examples such as slavery and segregation are prime examples. One reason the current system is unable to defend itself is its inability to prevent new and unexpected threats. This allows extremists to think up new abuses and provides them with useful loopholes.

This has had far-reaching implications in American history. In the immediate aftermath of the Civil War, amendments were made to the United States Constitution as part of the country's reconstruction, designed to guarantee that everyone was treated equally. In response, the political extremists in the southern states passed several laws and regulations that thwarted these principles. They drastically reduced the effectiveness of the Reconstruction Amendments. To be sure, slavery was now illegal. However, a series of laws known as "Jim Crow" acted to limit this newfound freedom. It segregated the African American community and suppressed their votes. While very different from slavery, these laws continued racial oppression in a different guise.

The woke movement is yet another example of extremists using cracks within the current system to their advantage. Proponents of woke ideology have passed several laws that have violated or limited human rights: these include violations or limits on things like freedom, mainly on the state level, that have limited freedom of speech, parental rights, and legalized forms of discrimination based on race or gender.

Another benefit of Ceidocratic government is that it eliminates extremists from using non-extremist policies to carry out extremist goals. Let's look at an example so this can be understood in greater detail. Enforcing immigration laws and implementing policies that do such is not extreme - as every nation needs these laws for the security of their citizens. However, an extremist who holds right-wing racist views, if allowed to participate in the political process and is put in executive office, might not implement an extremist policy like explicitly banning individuals of certain ethnicities from entering the country, or only deporting members of a certain racial group. But they could use their authority as the executive to target certain racial groups for deportation in immigration enforcement more than others, or banning individuals from certain communities from coming in under the disguise of national security, or use other tactics to target specific ethnic or racial groups that are not on paper or officially racist. However in the end, their goal is still achieved, they are discriminating against certain groups based on race or ethnicity.

On the other hand, a left-wing or revenge-racist might not explicitly state or implement a policy discriminating against or favoring particular racial groups for university admission. However they can implement certain policies or social programs that could indirectly lower the requirements or favor particular individuals of certain backgrounds based on race. The policy, not necessarily discriminatory, the end goal of discrimination, still achieved.

For too long, the woman's body has been under occupation by an extremist patriarchy. A Ceidocratic form of government will liberate her, empower her, and re-implement her absolute power, her absolute authority over her temple, and ensure that no hypocritical right-wing extremist, who preaches about individual liberty and individual rights, will be able to violate her right, by invading her bodily autonomy ever again.

A Ceidocratic government would end the campaign of demasculinization. The rephrasing of the masculine energy that built this great nation as toxic, the relabeling of the masculine traits of valor and courage that defend this nation as too aggressive, this redefining of strength as weakness, all this would come to an end. A Ceidocratic government would end this revenge sexist assault on men and boys, and masculinity would be given its rightful respect once again.

Our entire system is founded on the principles of freedom, human rights, and equality. However, there are so many cracks and loopholes in the system, that it has become impossible to protect them adequately. A Ceidocratic Government would focus on correcting this problem. Using its strong powers, it would prevent the implementation of ideas that threaten our freedoms.

Protection of the Fundamental Ideology While Abiding by Democracy

Liberal democracies have difficulty protecting their fundamental ideology. Unlike many other forms of government, they are not despotic or intolerant. Because their ideology guarantees freedom of speech, freedom of expression, and freedom of thought, even ideas that conflict with democracy and liberalism are allowed to thrive in a liberal inspired free society.

A free society is based on full equality and underlying fairness. Yet racism continues to flourish. It is thriving in its traditional and revenge forms. That is a pattern in our history from when slavery was legal, to today, when certain U.S. states have passed discriminatory laws. In addition, there have been challenges to freedom of speech as laws censoring speech have been passed in Europe and the United States. That is a violation of one of the most basic principles of democracy.

This is a significant weakness that democratic nations suffer. Individuals who hold ideals contrary to democracy (or extremists) can use it to manipulate the system, participate in, and influence the political system to their ends, such as the Nazis in the Weimar Republic, or Brazil today. There is a danger that Woke and Right-Wing extremists in the United States and Europe will do the same.

The advantage of a Ceidocracy is in its ability to abide by the principles of liberal democracy. It is uniquely suited to the task of upholding freedom of thought, expression, and speech.

It does allow extremists to express their fanatic ideas, which is their right. But it doesn't allow them to implement or carry them out. After all, their political program is based on violating others' rights. By limiting anti-democratic actions, Ceidocracy checks against extremist rule. It also protects the marketplace of ideas through a system that decentralizes the expression of thought while simultaneously ensuring that no one can exploit that openness to undermine the system itself.

Imagine a future in which you no longer have to fear extremists being elected to office, implementing racially motivated immigration policies, enacting measures that strip women of their dignity and rights, or separating families and deporting hard-working asylum seekers. A future where parents no longer have to worry about their children being taken by the state, where they can send their kids to school without fear of them being coerced into changing their sexual identity.

Ceidocracy guarantees such a future. It promises a government in which no congressman, president, or any other government official will ever be able to go against the will of the people. It strips away the power that this small minority of extremists currently holds in our nation. It promises that during elections, even if your candidate doesn't win, you don't have to worry about someone taking office who would implement authoritarianism, violate human rights, or disregard the Constitution as we see on both the extremist left and right today. It ensures that only centrist, center-left, and center-right candidates - heroes of the people - would prevail. In this future, you no longer have to fear extremism in your government. It ensures a government of the people, by the people, and for the people.

CHAPTER 4:

Addressing the Critiques

There is only one question that truly matters: will this work in reality? To be sure, there are problems and potential weaknesses. Two significant ones could touch on who gets labeled an extremist and whether that brush is used too broadly or narrowly. There is also the very real danger that the relevant extremism agency will turn into an authoritarian one or will be used as a political weapon by those in power. Without addressing these concerns, it is doubtful this plan will get off the ground.

To address the first concern, our definition of "extremist" is a critical safeguard. For legal purposes, extremists are people who hold ideals or beliefs that call for the violation of others' rights. Therefore, any individual who advances prejudicial views against a particular group, or does not tolerate opinions contrary to theirs. It is not that difficult to identify individuals who express these views, especially when they join extremist organizations.

It's important to emphasize that this system targets only individuals whose beliefs or actions clearly violate the rights of others. It is not intended to suppress dissenting or unconventional opinions. Therefore, the relevant agency must operate under clear, transparent criteria. It would ensure due process and safeguard against arbitrary or unjust targeting. A fully transparent appeal system would also be required.

But even with these safeguards, it can be challenging to limit the potential authoritarian pitfalls of Ceidocracy. That would require a careful differentiation between executive, legislative, and judicial power. That is a difficult task, since there has always been a level of ambiguity between what constitutes executive, legislative, and judicial power in the United States. There are several essential landmark cases unpacking these problems. For example, Youngstown Sheet & Tube Co. v. Sawyer (1952) and Dred Scott v. Sandford (1857).

The problems presented by separation of powers can be taxing. However, it remains an essential component in American democracy. The balance does not work perfectly. But the alternative, the domination of one arm of government, is immeasurably worse. The centralization of power has led to the worst abuses humanity has seen. Humanity knows from bitter experience that nothing is more dangerous than the concentration of authority in too few hands.

Ceidocracy holds the advantages of the separation of powers. In most cases, identifying extremist individuals and ideologies will not be that difficult. However, challenges will arise in some instances. Still, the system is practical and the alternatives are awful. The country is on a seemingly inexorable slide to division and dysfunction. If this system is not implemented, the slide towards division, dysfunction, and economic uncertainty will continue. It will destroy our way of life. The Ceidocratic system offers a way out.

The concern that the government agency specializing in extremism enforcement might act in an authoritarian manner is serious. However, it does not survive scrutiny. This will not threaten the system of checks and balances. Quite the contrary. Since extremism threatens the system, curtailing it will ensure that the checks and balances will operate more smoothly. Therefore, fears that this enforcement mechanism will become the American equivalent of the SS in Nazi Germany, or the KGB in the Soviet Union, are unfounded.

The agency will, of course, be subject to all laws and limitations of the American system, concerning its internal affairs, as well as to the courts and other law enforcement agencies. Most important of all, it will be subject to the ultimate and supreme law of the United States: the Constitution. Indeed, the operations and powers of this agency would not be materially different from those of existing federal agencies. But while the FBI specializes in federal law enforcement and organized crime, the DEA in drug enforcement, and the US Marshals in fugitive apprehension, this agency specializes in crimes of extremism.

Another potential objection to this system is that it is based on an undemocratic idea, of depriving people of their right to participate in the democratic process. That is a valid concern. But it should be tested on the results. The outcome will be a more democratic system than the one we currently live under. Remember who we are excluding from the process. Extremist individuals who believe in the violation of human rights and hold intolerant views. Their removal from the electoral process will protect the system. Some people wish to subvert democracy from within, as Hitler did in Germany and Putin did in Russia. This will help prevent that.

The Ceidocratic approach is not a panacea. The problems our society faces will not be entirely fixed by it. But its core premise, the exclusion of extremists, is a new gain for democracy. It does not present a threat. Instead, it offers much-needed protection. The risks of overreach are real. But they apply to all uses of executive power. The system of checks and balances will help protect against excesses. In addition, if the definitions of extremism are rigorously maintained, abuses will be reliably prevented. Ceidocracy will defend democratic values. Even if it is not perfect, the alternative is to permit extremists to exploit the openness of democracy. That is the actual danger.

CHAPTER 5:

A Government Abiding by Universal Law

The principles that make centrism essential in politics - balance, moderation, and equilibrium - are reflected in the very fabric of the universe. Reality itself operates according to universal laws, fundamental principles that are absolute, objective, and unchanging. These laws govern everything consistently, regardless of human beliefs or opinions. Everything from the largest galaxies to the smallest quantum systems - to consciousness itself is dictated by these laws that formulate reality. These laws make up the constitution of the universe.

The Ceidocratic form of government is inspired by and abides by universal laws. When I discuss the universal laws, it can evoke a spiritual or religious form of universalism, which assigns spiritual or religious meaning to certain universal principles. But that is not the meaning of universal law in this context. While this field is related and has intriguing ideas, I am referring instead to the ever-growing field of academic or scientific universalism.

The scientific study of universal principles relies on identifying laws or truths that hold across multiple aspects of reality. If these hold across consciousness, information, mathematics, and the physical world, they can be considered universal laws that apply throughout the universe and in all forms of reality.

One of these laws is the Law of Polarity, also known as the Law of Balance or Equilibrium. This is an objective truth that holds across all aspects of reality. Every element or system of reality naturally seeks a state of balance or equilibrium, driven by opposing forces that together create a stable state. In the physical sciences, this can be seen in atoms: protons and electrons are two opposing forces whose interaction stabilizes atomic systems.

Mathematics offers a good example of how this works. The Law of Polarity appears in several key areas. One instance is the number line and additive inverses. Every number has an opposite, its additive inverse. For example, the additive inverse of +5 is -5, and their sum equals zero, representing equilibrium. Vectors are another area where polarity is evident. Every vector V has an opposite vector pointing in the opposite direction. When added together, these two vectors equal the zero vector - the point of balance with no net direction or magnitude. Thus, the principle that two opposing variables can combine to form an equilibrium holds in this realm as well.

Similar principles apply in economics, a field that studies human behavior and decision-making. The most basic concept in this discipline is supply and demand. The assumption, borne out by reality, is that markets naturally seek a state of equilibrium. The force of supply, fueled by the motivation to sell products or services for maximum profit, and the opposing force of demand, driven by the impulse to acquire goods at the lowest cost, balance one another. The interaction forms an equilibrium point where the two opposing forces meet. This principle holds across both microeconomic markets and broader economic systems.

We have only scratched the surface of systems and aspects of reality in which these laws of balance hold. Of course, the one most relevant to us is the realm of politics and government.

The Law of Polarity in Government

The American experiment has been an unrivaled success, the world's most successful democracy. However, it is not the most Democratic country in the world. In some ways, it is less democratic than many other nations today. Even ancient Athens was more democratic in some ways, though it did not allow women and enslaved people to vote. It is not, strictly speaking, the constitution, either. There have been other well crafted constitutions before and after the American founding, and those nations did not achieve the success of the United States. Instead, the secret is the way the country functions thanks to a uniquely balanced system.

An examination of the ideological or political compass demonstrates this point well. On the vertical axis, where the top represents concentrated authoritarian power and the bottom represents decentralized power spread across many individuals and institutions, the American system's most outstanding achievement is its position near the middle.

The American system is not overly authoritarian, and power is not excessively concentrated in the hands of any individual or institution. However, power is not excessively dispersed either. It maintains an equitable and functional balance.

Dispersed power systems, such as anarchies, direct democracies, and similar political structures, can tend toward instability or risk violations of rights and freedoms. Some ancient Greek city-states functioned as direct democracies, and they suffered from extensive polarization and infighting.

They also risk violating the rights of smaller or minority groups through the tyranny of the majority. Moving further downward to anarchies - exceptionally pure anarchies - tend to be the most unstable systems because there is little or no rule of law. Without legal checks or restraints, individuals can act without legal consequences. They could potentially violate the rights of others. Therefore, you could see an outsized number of individuals seizing property, engaging in vigilante justice, or threatening the right to life of other citizens. That is how anarchy can lead to chaos and societal dysfunction.

However, there are some exceptions. Some Swiss cantons have gone beyond the direct democracy of Greek city-states to develop pure democracy. Their success in specific categories of national achievement is partly due to rare societal attributes, such as a relatively small population, an unusual degree of social and cultural agreement, and other unique factors. It is hard to translate this to different cultures and impossible to replicate on a larger scale.

The problems with the authoritarian style of government are very well known. Autocracies, oligarchies, and other authoritarian systems have perpetrated some of the most nefarious instances of human rights violations. From the absolute monarchies of ancient times, to the fascist rule of the Nazis, to the communist regimes - sometimes called "evil empires" as Reagan referred to them - and to modern authoritarian governments like those of China, Russia, and Iran. Every one of these governments is guilty of the extensive violation of the rights of the people and they rule through fear and brutality.

Political systems with concentrated power are less unstable than those that disperse it. Nonetheless, they do tend to face instability. In many cases, the majority of people living under these systems may not be truly loyal to the government. They may not feel the same patriotism or motivation to use their talents for the betterment of their nation that individuals in freer societies often do. Therefore, these systems require constant efforts to prevent revolts. In China, the CCP allocates a massive portion of its budget to monitoring and surveilling its own people. That takes money and resources away from the military, welfare, and other areas. To be sure, there are exceptions to this rule. Some autocratic rulers have genuinely promoted the well being of their nations and protected the rights of individuals. But these instances are rare. There are no guardrails to prevent abuses and good leaders are often replaced by bad ones since the population has no input through the electoral process.

America is a republic under a democratic form of government. The balance that characterizes this system of government managed to avoid the dysfunction and instability of pure democracies or anarchies. Meanwhile it successfully avoids the harsh rule characteristic of authoritarian governments. It does so by allowing people to elect their representatives and placing checks on officials by holding them accountable to the electorate. At the same time, the system also limits the direct power of the people. While voters elect their representatives, they have little input into the day-to-day operations of the government.

The separation of powers is another aspect of the American system that brings equilibrium. The Executive, Legislative, and Judicial powers are separated, which decentralizes power. However, each of these branches still have significant institutional power, allowing them to make decisions, take actions, and possess powers as circumscribed by the constitution.

The federal system keeps the American system balanced at a point that is near the center of the political compass. Unlike a unitary system, where the central government has near-complete authority over the nation, and unlike a confederacy, where the states or local governments hold the majority of power, a federal system falls somewhere in between these extremes. A federal system has a stronger central government than a confederacy would. It provides the federal government with certain powers and the authority to enact laws that take precedence over local or regional laws, creating a more secure and unified nation. However, under this system, regional and local governments have powers and rights the federal government cannot infringe upon. That structure allows distinct local identities and rights to flourish, while still checking the power of the federal government.

The Constitution provides another vital limitation on government power. It ensures the authorities cannot impose laws that violate individual rights and freedoms.

This principle aligns with the Law of Polarity - a concept where two opposing forces, strong centralized power and its opposite, decentralized or dispersed power, meet and balance each other. The greatest achievement of the American system is the healthy balance of central and local power that it has achieved, by occupying an equilibrium at the center. This principle played a crucial role in the unrivaled success of the American experiment, helping establish it as one of the world's first and most successful democracies.

America effectively achieved equilibrium on the vertical power axis of the ideological compass, balancing centralized and decentralized power. To avoid the economic, political, or other forms of collapse that threaten our nation if nothing changes, we must now establish equilibrium on the horizontal, left-right ideological axis. This balance can be attained through a Ceidocratic form of government. Together with the system of checks and balances, Ceidocracy would also reinforce centrism along the vertical axis by limiting the influence of extremists - those with excessively authoritarian or anarchic views - from imposing non-democratic policies on society.

The extreme poles of the ideological compass are antithetical to each other. They meet and equilibrate at the center of the political map. That is why a democracy based on centrism is natural and upholds the principle of balance, a law of the universe. The removal of the unbalanced forces of extremism from the system ensures that the stable forces of centrism and common sense prevail. The political chaos of extreme right and left factions plaguing the American system today can be resolved. It can be replaced by a more secure political system that abides by the timeless truth of the universe: that stability and security can only be achieved through balance and moderation.

Conclusion

President Ronald Reagan once said, "We can preserve for our children this, the last best hope of man on Earth, or we can sentence them to take the last step into a thousand years of darkness."

At one time I firmly believed that our political system was invincible. As a result I predicted that our form of democracy is far too advanced to ever fall to the kind of authoritarianism that plagued Germany or Italy in the 20th century. Developments on the state level made it agonizingly clear that I was wrong.

Some of our nation's great states have become one-party states. Most U.S. states used to have even playing fields, fair elections. However, today it is tough for Republicans to compete in California or Democrats to compete in Texas. These states and others have used gerrymandering and other unscrupulous methods to gain an electoral advantage. The sum of this process is that it is almost impossible for anyone to compete with the dominant party in those states. This has made many states throughout America effectively one-party systems.

Even within the parties themselves, individuals who don't wholeheartedly adhere to the dominant extreme dogma are often effectively outcast and suppressed. I thought that if this is happening at the state level, there is a very high chance it will occur at the national level. I realized that a significant factor in this is the political polarity. The competition between two deadlocked parties, neither of which can take complete control of the political process.

Let's keep in mind what we are trying to protect and why. In the summer of 1787, the delegates of the federal convention finally completed their work, creating the most excellent and advanced constitution the world had ever seen. The result was a true masterpiece of human genius, cementing America's future as one of the greatest nations in human history. As the delegates left Independence Hall in Philadelphia, Elizabeth Willing Powel asked Benjamin Franklin, one of the nation's founding fathers, "Well, Doctor, what have we got? A republic or a monarchy?" Franklin's reply was brief but profound - one of the most memorable and wise statements in history. He said, "A republic - if you can keep it."

Franklin emphasized a timeless and valuable truth about the Republican form of government. The importance of this truth goes far beyond the confines of the American experiment. It is an underlying truth of reality itself.

One of the most well-known sayings in history is that you can't have your cake and eat it too - and it's famous for good reason. Why is it that extraordinary success always comes with a catch - greatness only up to a point, strength balanced by weakness, and perfection that hides a flaw? Even the fictional characters in our culture face this truth. Superman has nearly limitless strength but suffers from a slight weakness: kryptonite. Darth Vader was the most powerful user of the Force in Star Wars, but he was also the most emotionally vulnerable and unstable. This idea dates back to ancient times, as reflected in stories such as Achilles' heel and Samson's strength tied to his hair.

It is a fundamental truth of reality that success comes at a price and that strength is only acquired through pain. Even the best-known celebrities cannot escape this truth. It is a law of reality that no matter how much you acquire or how successful you become, there will always be something lacking. No matter how strong you are, some weakness will hold you back.

This truth holds in the political sphere. Liberal democracies, particularly constitutional republics like the United States, are without question the most successful form of government in human history. They brought about unprecedented technological advancement, while generating unimaginable wealth. They also shape a more loyal and patriotic people than any other. After all, it is a system of the people and for the people and personally benefits each and every individual to a greater degree than any other regime.

Despite the unrivaled success enjoyed by societies under these forms of government, political and social divisions and instability plague them.

President Reagan, one of America's greatest leaders, once said, "Freedom is never more than one generation away from extinction." Today it seems even closer. We are on the cusp of two potential but equally catastrophic tragedies: America becoming a totalitarian extremist system dominated by one party, or a total political, economic and societal collapse.

We are in one of the worst situations our country has faced, and we may not find a way out. Americans are not used to being in a situation where things do not seem to be improving. Rather than getting better, the problem continues to worsen.

We face a seemingly endless mountain of problems. If our fracturing political system doesn't collapse because of political disunity, and if our weakened economy doesn't collapse because of inflation and the unprecedented national debt, then democracy itself faces ruin through a complete takeover of our political system and the implementation of an authoritarian one-party state. The United States could become a country that kidnaps its children and violates parental rights. Or it could discriminate against and violate the rights of America's most vulnerable communities like

LGBTQ. It can increase its efforts in separating immigrant families or support traditional or revenge forms of racism and discrimination.

America was founded on ideals of common sense. It was created to safeguard centrism, and not to promote the extremism of the far left or the far right. Liberalism, free speech, and checks and balances are core democratic ideals that belong to centrism - not the far left or the far right. Centrism is not despotic or intolerant; it is open-minded and inclusive. It is not particularist but democratic. It benefits not just the rich but also does not steal individuals' hard-earned wages through redistribution. It is economically competent, honoring free-market principles - generating the massive wealth that comes from market capitalism while also using that wealth to assist the less fortunate. This is just as the great economist Adam Smith intended capitalism to do; he knew that capitalism is the only system capable of generating the wealth necessary to help the less fortunate. Centrism is a perfectly balanced system. Its application is why the American experiment has worked so well and blossomed into one of the most successful democracies in the world.

These principles of centrism are where we find the future of this country. If we return to them, we can build a country that is not despotic or intolerant. Instead, we will move toward an open-minded and inclusive future - one that is not particularist but democratic, a system that does not benefit just the rich but also does not steal the hard-earned wages of individuals to redistribute them. A centrist society that is economically competent and honors free-market principles - the same principles that have generated massive wealth for generations and used those gains to assist the less fortunate.

While our system was built on centrist principles, it has not applied them perfectly or evenly. If our nation had been a true centrist ideological democracy all along, our nation would have been spared the taint of slavery, the years of pain and social unrest that accompanied the civil rights movement, discrimination against African-Americans and other minorities, and the continuous violation of women's rights.

If America had a government that could filter out radical extremists, we would have avoided the unjust discrimination whites experience through reverse racism in certain parts of America, we would have avoided the demasculinization of young men as a result of reverse sexism, and we would have saved thousands of young minors from sex change surgeries and sterilization - procedures they are too young to consent to.

If we want to take back our nation, we must unite. We must mobilize to stop the two small groups of radical extremists in power, who currently determine the destiny of our country, of our communities, and hold the fate of our families in their hands. We must declare that this is not their nation - it is ours!

I know there is a hard road ahead. I understand that every third-party option has had either no or very little success. I am fully aware of the mountain of obstacles that come with challenging such a robust system of special interests made up of the most powerful corporations and politicians.

But no truly outstanding achievement has ever been easily attained. Humanity's greatest accomplishments were achieved through pain, hard work, and unwavering determination to overcome the greatest obstacles. It was not easy to fight the most powerful military force in the world during the American Revolution, fighting the Civil War was not easy, nor was the struggle for civil rights. Taking on fascist tyranny during World War II and fighting for women's rights was not easy either. But in the end, the pain, the suffering, the hard work, the insults, the beatings in the streets and attacks by dogs and the lives lost were worth it.

If you refuse to take action because it is complex or too difficult, if you become passive or complacent, then you render the sacrifice and hard work of those brave men and women who have gotten us this far as a nation meaningless. You disregard the legacies on which our society stands today - King, Tubman, Washington, Lincoln, Wollstonecraft, Yousafzai, and the countless others who shed their blood defending our ideals on the battlefield. By doing so, you risk rendering their sacrifice futile.

Ask yourself how history will judge us if we did not take action despite having a massive advantage in numbers over these two small groups of extremists? What side of history are you on if you know these fanatics are violating the rights of your fellow Americans, your neighbors in your community, your family members, but you refused to stand up for them because the obstacles were too significant?

You must raise your voice. You need to revolt against this anti-democratic system. Stand up for what you believe in, and say no. Say no to immigration policies that separate families and make husbands and fathers disappear. Reject policies that violate parental rights. Take a stand to defend young children from sexual mutilation and abuse. Say no to policies that violate a woman's ownership of her own body. Above all, stand firm against extremism!

We are in dark times. From the geopolitical situation unfolding across the globe to the domestic problems we face here at home, chaos and uncertainty reign supreme. For too long, American voters have had no real option but to choose between two extremes - neither of which truly represents them nor genuinely holds their ideals and interests at heart.

The Biden era of America was defined by reverse racism and discrimination unleashed on a scale never seen before; by widespread violations of parental rights; by attacks on children through coerced sex reidentification - both psychological and physical; by assaults on free speech; and by high inflation and economic decline.

The Trump era, by contrast, is defined by authoritarianism; by unprecedented levels of police brutality; and by ICE operations that target not only violent illegal criminals but also peaceful asylum seekers and, in some cases, American citizens themselves. Policies under Trump further accelerate climate change in an already unstable environment. Despite promises of economic prosperity, the so-called "one big beautiful bill" has massively increased the national debt, fueling deeper economic insecurity and long-term fiscal instability.

It is time to reignite this beacon - this great nation of human genius - so that we may look toward a future of light rather than darkness, so that young boys and girls can hold their heads up high once again, so that their little hearts can wander, discover, and dream, and let that organ of passion lead them into a future of greatness. It is time to begin a new era in America: one defined by centrism and common sense, rejecting both the unreasonable extremes of the left and the harsh bigotry of the right.

An era for all Americans - for women and men; for Latinos, for Blacks, for Whites; for asylum seekers and Dreamers alike. An era of economic security and prosperity for citizens of every background. A time defined not by bigotry, nor by revenge for past hardships for which no one alive today is responsible, but by unity and love.

An era of Ceidocracy.

www.ingramcontent.com/pod-product-compliance
Lightning Source LLC
LaVergne TN
LVHW011048110826
845149LV00015B/3404